Alternative Altars

Chicago History of
American Religion

A Series Edited by
Martin E. Marty

Alternative Altars
*Unconventional
and Eastern
Spirituality
in America*

Robert S. Ellwood, Jr.

The University of Chicago Press Chicago and London

ROBERT S. ELLWOOD, JR., is Bishop James W. Bashford Professor of Oriental Studies in the School of Religion of the University of Southern California. He is the author of numerous scholarly books and articles.

The University of Chicago Press, Chicago 60637
The University of Chicago Press, Ltd., London
© 1979 by The University of Chicago
All rights reserved. Published 1979
Printed in the United States of America
83 82 81 80 79   5 4 3 2

Library of Congress Cataloging in Publication Data

Ellwood, Robert S.   1933–
    Alternative Altars

    (Chicago history of American religion)
    Includes bibliographical references and index.
    1. United States—Religion—1945-   2. Cults—
United States.   1. Title.
BL2530.U6E44   200'.973   78-15089
ISBN 0-226-20618-1

Contents

Foreword

At the far edges of my bookshelves on American religious history are a number of titles that put the subject of this book in its place: *Strange Sects and Curious Cults, Strange Sects and Cults, Those Curious New Cults, New Gods in America, The New Religions, Faiths for the Few.* Some scholars estimate the number of people attracted to these groups as anywhere from two to twenty million, and millions more—especially if we include devotees of astrology and the occult—see something in what they represent, even if these interested people do not join cults to express their faith.

What makes sects and cults "strange," and "curious," and why are they "new" for the "few"?

First, the story of these groups violates a kind of canon that for over a century American religious historians have used to define the boundaries of respectability for their readers. No one chartered them to put narrow boundaries around their story or their subjects; these authors simply reflected the viewpoints of their sponsors and clienteles, and thus unofficially established certain faiths as non-strange or non-curious because they seemed old and belonged to the many. A review of this canonical sense will help prepare readers for the current book.

Because New England was the cultural center of the nineteenth-century churches and because the early New Englanders were careful to speak clearly and to leave plenty of documents, New England was at the heart of the story of mainstream religion. The generous early authors gave some weight to the contributions of Virginians, while they treated Rhode Islanders and Pennsylvanians as "strange" and "curious." Eventually these dissenters and mavericks from those colonies won their way and historians charitably enlarged the canon to include with favor all "evangelical" Protestants. The first major book in the canon, *Religion in America* by Robert Baird, used such a line of discrimination. The "unevangelicals" were "Atheists, Deists, Socialists, Fourrierists [sic], Rappists, Shakers, Mormons, Swedenborgians, Tunkers," and, less strange and curious, Catholics, Unitarians, Christ-ians, Universalists, and Jews.

Decades later the historians included all Protestantism in their informal canon until, after a century of Catholic growth, William Warren Sweet began to include Catholics in *The Story of Religion in America,* though as late as 1950 he was still paying at best grudging attention in his best-seller and norm-setter to all non-Protestants. In the decades since, most historians have come to include Catholics and Jews, thus setting up "biblical religion" as *the* American religion. Meanwhile, they have also paid some attention to the equally respectable tradition of the religion of Enlightenment, called variously the "religion of the republic," civil religion, or, in Benjamin Franklin's useful phrase, "publick religion." The most expansive histories—the best is Sydney E. Ahlstrom's *A Religious History of the American People*—included segregated chapters on the subjects Ellwood treats. Ahlstrom, for example, has as his sixty-first chapter: "Piety for the Age of Aquarius: Theosophy, Occultism, and Non-Western Religion." No one else pushed the edges of the canon as far as he, but Ahlstrom remained clear about one theme: Puritanism provided the thread for the story until the 1960s, and when it unraveled, the story became less clear.

The second reason why the groups here scrutinized are considered strange and curious has to do with the fact that the American majority tends to establish a world view and to gain plausibility for it even among those who do not accept the faith. To a complete outsider the traditional faiths may look as arcane and idiosyncratic as the "marginal" ones do. I have heard middle-class Americans chuckle when told of Melanesian Cargo Cults, groups of people who in colonial times and even after World War II developed an elaborate mythology to explain why the whites of the world seemed prosperous and they were not—yet. As American or Japanese troops landed with abundant supplies on their islands, the tribespeople explained that their own ancestors would come back at an end of an age to redeem them, bringing along endless bounty for the once-deprived people.

What of the laughers? Some of them adhered to the outlook of the most notable evangelist of our age. He was an intimate of five presidents, the most admired man of his decades, according to the polls. Yet he propagated the idea that some time suddenly and soon a man who lived two thousand years ago would literally return to earth and reign for a thousand years, and that accompanying his return would be a great world-ending battle in the Middle East. Few thought this "curious." Others of the amused were Roman Catholics, Lutherans, or Episcopalians, who gathered weekly to receive a little flattened piece of white bread and a taste of wine, believing that therewith they were eating the flesh and drinking the blood of their God, communing with him "until he comes again." Few others thought *them* unrespectable, as indeed they were not, because their faith had established itself, while those faiths considered strange and curious had not. Yet their beliefs functioned for these evangelicals and catholics the way cargo cults worked for the Melanesians—or the way the "new" faiths work for millions of the "few."

Robert S. Ellwood, Jr., is not out to violate the sensibilities of those of us who believe in the classic biblical faiths of the Western world; indeed, he shares one of those faiths himself. Instead, his purpose is to enlarge the concept and contents of the canon, to extend the boundaries that define the plausible and the acceptable, if not the respectable, and to give an honest accounting—always the first task of the historian—of movements or people who leave their mark on a populace.

Many of us have come to speak of the spiritual phenomena that come into Ellwood's scope as "new." But some of them quite possibly antedate biblical religion and certainly are older than Christianity. They are believed by most people to be new to American shores. Of course, they had a history in America before the boom in the seventies. In the conventional telling—and I am among the conventional tellers—the religions of the East or the occult first showed up in Salem witchcraft and then, more respectably, as the "Yankee Hindoo" emphasis of Ralph Waldo Emerson and Henry David Thoreau. After this a few strange people turned to spiritualism and others followed a mysterious woman into Theosophy, but not until the World's Parliament of Religions in 1893, when representatives of Hinduism and Zen Buddhism showed up at Chicago, did citizens have any close contact with Eastern faiths. While there was always an occult underground, in the 1930s a number of English authors, Aldous Huxley chief among them, began to import "the perennial philosophy." Finally in the 1950s came the Zen and "beat" poets, and in the late 1960s the flowering of spiritualities that have left their imprint on the whole nation.

Ellwood retraces that history, but shows that it was never quite as marginal as this telling suggests. Rather than taking readers through a kind of curiosity shop, he wisely chooses to concentrate on three narratives or case studies and, by his sustained focus on them, to raise most of the issues that have to do with "emergent" and "excursus" spirituality. It is likely that readers will be more aware than before of its emergence and less likely than ever to think of it as a *mere* excursus from the mainstream of American religiosity. Here, instead, is a book that raises questions for a society that is progressively losing its canon, its norm, its traditional religions by which others are measured. Professor Ellwood is less concerned with answering those questions than with providing readers with the data base and perspective on which to do their own thinking and resolving.

MARTIN E. MARTY
THE UNIVERSITY OF CHICAGO

Preface

This essay began as a study of "non-normative religion" in America. I have changed the terms to ones more positive and, I hope, more illuminating in connotation. But the original definition of the task remains: to investigate religious life in this country outside the Judeo-Christian mainstream and its significance for American spiritual culture.

Readers aware of the marshy terrain such a quest is likely to enter may first ask what definition of religion undergirds it. The one at the back of my mind is relatively elaborate and restrictive. I am not thinking of religion simply in light of an existential definition, such as Paul Tillich's "ultimate concern," but also as a cultural system, in Clifford Geertz's sense, and as an expression of a social construction of reality in the meaning of Berger and Luckmann.

We will be concerned with socially reified religion which, through an orchestration of concepts, rites, and groups that involve but transcend the individual, formally offers models of meaning-giving ultimate reality and ways of access to it. A good "handle" for dealing with religion in this way is to analyze it in terms of the three forms of religious expression of the phenomenological sociologist of religion Joachim Wach. While accepting that at its core religion involves a numinous, transcendent, or existential reality, Wach indicated that its visible phenomena appear through three forms: the theoretical, the concepts and paradigmatic narratives; the practical, the praxis of rites, prayer, meditation, pilgrimage, services, gestures; the sociological, or its articulation in groups, leadership, and interpersonal relations. My preference is to restrict the use of the word "religion" to that highly visible and discrete class of human phenomena which has an ultimate reference *and* has interlocking expressions in all three of these forms. Thus, we will not be especially concerned with ideas without sociological structures and some kind of praxis to go with them, nor with groups without transcendent ideas.

I am well aware that some of the movements to be discussed do not think that the word religion appropriately applies to them and do not use it of themselves. This is a point of view which I respect and which at some periods, or from some perspectives, I would agree is valid. In connection with them I have often used a term other than religion, such as spirituality. Nonetheless, I think that as a formal definition the foregoing concept of religion allows us to separate out sociologically reified spirituality from purely intellectual movements.

In approaching this task, I early decided not to attempt a fullblown historical survey of non-normative religion. Rather, I have chosen here to focus major attention on theoretical models for understanding American non-normative spirituality, and, by way of illustration, to examine in depth three movements—or, rather, three moments in the lives of three movements. They are, however, movements of immense significance, and ones which well encapsulate three eras in its history: Spiritualism, Theosophy, and American Zen. I trust that this method, far from being disappointingly restrictive, will cast some fresh light on the whole spiritual scene outside the mainstream.

Finally, I would like to add a personal note. Often disquisitions on social movements manage to seem inhumanly dispassionate, if not condescending. They may also seem to communicate less respect for the ideas which have inspired them than concern for the human foibles and frailties, and the historical vicissitudes, which have beset them as they have all human institutions and endeavors. Yet there is a place for both the social commentator and the philosopher; as Swedenborg and the Zen sages have taught, compassion and wisdom are ultimately two sides of the same reality and need each other for completion . . . let the human perspective lead to the first, and philosophy to wisdom. I myself have a high regard for what has been brought to America by much of the non-normative spiritual tradition. I have benefited immensely from reading Shaker, Swedenborgian, and Spiritualist literature; I am a member of the Theosophical Society in America, as well as an Episcopal clergyman; I have studied and practiced Zen meditation, art, and life fairly extensively. But the expounding of all of that would make a different book than this one.

Finally, I would like to express deep gratitude to those who have assisted with this project. The Pulitzer Prize-winning poet Gary Snyder read the chapter on American Zen, in which he is a major figure, and made several very useful comments and corrections. The full manuscript was read by Professor James T. Richardson, of the Department of Sociology of the University of Nevada; by Professor Bruce Campbell, visiting scholar at the Institute of Religious Studies, University of California, Santa Barbara, and an authority on Theosophical history; by Professor William LaFleur, of the Department of Religious Studies, Princeton University; by Professor Catherine Albanese, Department of Religion, Wright State University, Dayton, Ohio; and by Professor Martin E. Marty, of the University of Chicago Divinity School, editor of the series in which this book appears. Their advice and help, often given with a generosity that went far beyond the call of duty, has made this book considerably better than it would otherwise have been. For those failings that remain, the author takes full responsibility.

1   Perspectives

1

Temple and Cave in America

Two American Churches

Not far from where I live, a quiet, shady street runs through a small suburban town. On one side of that street, as on hundreds of shady streets in as many American small towns, a large Methodist church complex rises. Over the landscaped grounds sprawl sanctuary, offices, auditoria, parking lots, and countless classrooms. The solidity and evident prosperity of this edifice proclaim that it is a local manifestation of the proper, legitimate, respectable religion of the land, akin in that sense to Canterbury Cathedral in England, or the Altar of Heaven of the old Chinese emperors in Peking.

Looking at this substantial place of worship, a keen observer might notice, out of the corners of his eyes, something else across the street. There a modest house has been converted into another sort of shrine. If the visitor were to examine it, he would see that its living room has been lovingly but amateurishly redecorated to make the sanctuary. Its single meeting room was formerly the garage. Much of the lawn has become a miniscule parking lot. In front, a crude sign proudly carries the legend, "First United Spiritualist Church." Behind this simple title and shabby facade lay realms of sacred mystery and marvel undreamed by those whose God is content to remain on the other side of the street.

A former minister of this Spiritualist church, an American shaman if ever there was one—other than Native American medicine men with memories of authentic vision quests—relates a call that was no Wesleyan warm-hearted experience. He says that long ago, on a freezing midwinter night in an Illinois farm-

1

house, a kindly Indian spirit guide brought him the tangible spirit of a little neighbor girl whom he had not even known had died that same night. She wanted to communicate that all was well with her on the Other Side.

Now, in the former garage converted into a seance room, twice a week this old habitue of two worlds went into trance and, assisted by four familiar guides, delivered messages from Spirit.

I have attended a fair number of seances in that place, and can attest to their unfailing fascination. On one occasion when my wife was with me, one of the guides—a garrulous American Indian spirit—professed to go into our home (which the medium had never visited) and describe what he saw. There were some misses, but a few items, including a broken lamp, were striking hits. We later calculated about 75 percent accuracy.

More intriguing was the audience of some twenty persons, all of whom received personal messages. The majority seemed not to be members of the church; a few may even have had their official connection across the street. One or two were somewhat familiar with occultism and talked knowingly of chakras and planes and the like. The majority were clearly from blue-collar families and had many hard years behind them. They clung eagerly to words from Spirit regarding deceased loved ones, and advice about travel, sickness, or errant sons and spouses.

Once I attended a "materialization seance" at the same site. A visiting Spiritualist minister from another state was the officiant. He first entered the "cabinet," a closetlike affair with curtains in the corner of the room, and allegedly went into a trance which enabled something of his vital substance—"ectoplasm"—to leave the body and provide material out of which spirits could take ethereal but visible shape.

Then, the room almost totally darkened, there emerged from the cabinet a series of apparitions in willowy spectral garb, from little girls to ancient kings, all bearing messages to various members of the bemused circle. One of the first to appear was the shade of Nelson Eddy, who sang a vibrant rendition of "In the Sweet Bye-and-Bye." The revenant of my mentor on the inner planes, a one-time officer of Caesar, appeared and presented me with an alleged old Roman coin as a token of his authenticity; I still keep it in my desk.

But the magical mood of communication between worlds and centuries was broken toward the end of the evening when a young man of proletarian accent, a skeptic in limbo, arose to proclaim he had "seen enough phoney spooks." He flashed on a cigarette lighter and two trousered legs were suddenly clearly visible beneath the current specter floating about the chamber. That figure beat a hasty retreat into the cabinet.

Shortly thereafter the medium stumbled out of the same place, rubbing his eyes and asking what had happened. When he was informed, he asserted that he could have been killed by such a shock to his vital substance when it was out of his body in the form of ectoplasm. He then and there departed whence he had come. The regular minister of the church—whom I respect as a devout Spiritualist divine—entered the tense, muttering room to refund apologetically to each of us the five-dollar "donation" we had made to attend this performance and to request us to leave immediately. He said something about the sort of mediums who give Spiritualism a bad name. But because I considered the evening well worthwhile as entertainment and edification, I was reluctant to accept the refund.

Peter Berger has written that "religion is man's audacious attempt to see the whole universe as humanly significant."[1] There were, to be sure, several audacious elements evident in the little Spiritualist church on that gaudy night. (For that matter, an omniscient eye might have detected audacious features in the quieter church across the street as well.) But I also felt there a desperate attempt to wrench from the infinitely dumb but numinous universe around us, by whatever forcing and contrivance, a human significance. However the living lie, the dead do not die: that heavy certitude I have felt thick as sour cream in the air of every Spiritualist meeting I have attended.

Of course, a comparable affirmation of eternal life could probably also be found in the sprawling, shiny "mainline" church. But its intimations of immortality are presented in a different atmosphere. If it is at all typical of the Middle American Protestantism the building suggests, the Sunday morning rite in the church across the street is not difficult to evoke. A moment's stillness, and one's mind echoes with hymns like "This Is My Father's World," with the sonorous words of scripture, the compassionate pastoral prayer, the announcements of youth group hayrack rides and basketball games, of committee meetings and pancake suppers. The sermon would be warm with the affirmation of honesty, love, and under-standing. Then, the coffee hour, the gathering-up of children from the far-flung reaches of the Sunday school, the ranchwagons and sedans loaded again, long Sunday dinners in a hundred homes, and finally TVs turned to pro football.

The Temple Paradigm

If there is a paradigm for the "mainline" church style of religion, surely it is the temple which Solomon built in Jerusalem when all was at peace, in that city whose ideal form has always suggested men dwelling together like brothers in happy and holy harmony, full of gratitude to God for fruitful families and bounteous fields. Individual and state, heaven and earth, visibly become seamless unities, all people accepting the "natural orders" and the stan-dard, official dispensations of grace as the way things are. No dark, quizzical places linger in a man's soul where he wonders if all this is only pretending, and if the apparent promises of God are not always what they seem.

Instead, the people all joined with the sage king in saying at the temple's dedication, "Blessed be the Lord who has given his people Israel rest, as he promised; not one of the promises he made through his servant Moses has failed." One reads on: "So Solomon and all Israel with him, a great assembly from Lebohamath to the Torrent of Egypt, celebrated the pilgrim-feast at that time before the Lord our God for seven days. On the eighth day he dismissed the people; and they blessed the king and went home happy and glad at heart for all the prosperity granted by the Lord to his servant David and his people Israel." (1 Kings 8:56, 65-66)

The Cave Paradigm

Another paradigm has also haunted the West through the millen-nia, and that is Plato's famous image of the Cave. In it mankind is portrayed, not as a happy community rejoicing in God's peace and bounty, but as prisoners fettered in a cavern. The entry to the cave is open to the light, but the prisoners are shackled so they can only face the other way. All they know of reality is a shadowplay created by a bonfire behind them, before which bearers carry trees and human forms to cast shadows before the deprived eyes of the captives, who, thinking these poor penumbras are the real things, give them names and talk about them.

And, the philosopher continues, suppose one of the denizens of the cave were by some mortal or immortal force to be dragged from his place and taken out into full sunlight. Suppose he were thrust into light even greater that that which threw the pitiful shadows—how would he react?

At first the solar brilliance would hurt his eyes, and he would want nothing more than to retreat back to the comforting darkness of the cave. Yet when he did return, he would be as one blessed by a wisdom the others had never known or had forgotten—though he would also be so bedazzled and befuddled by the ultimate light that he would *seem* even more stupid and benighted than they.

Cave and Temple

The parable of the cave may serve as a paradigm for an opposite style of religious life from that of the temple. The cave image was itself inspired by those initiatory mysteries—Eleusis, Orphism—which stood apart from the sunny parthenons of Greek civic religion to which the leading men of the community led bullocks on festive days.

The temple and the cave remind us that all through the world's religions the communal temple and the initiatory mystery, in one guise or another, stand facing each other. We shall refer to the "temple" style as "established religion" and the "cave" style as "emergent religion." The latter, in an individual, will be called "excursus religion." Every society has its great official and popular fanes which demarcate the official recognition of deity: the huge mosques of Cairo or Teheran, the Grand Shrine of Ise in Japan, the cathedrals of Europe. In these houses of established religion worship is vast, sweeping, impersonal, aesthetically pleasing. The clergy are polished and well-educated, the sermons smoothly phrased and intellectually sophisticated. Here mayors and heads of state are pleased to be seen, and here wholesome families gather to honor births and deaths and to celebrate the public ceremonies of their people.

This is the temple, like Solomon's. It is the "church" of Ernst Troeltsch's sociology of religion. Hierarchical and professional in leadership, but inclusive in membership, established religion embraces all within a society who have not made a deliberate, self-conscious choice to be something else or do not happen to be hereditary members of a small deviant group. Established religion ordinarily upholds the normative values of the society—even moderately "worldly" values—either explicitly, or implicitly through the example of the lifestyle of its leadership and prominent members. It may have a formal creedal orthodoxy and rigorous moral ideals, but it does not make stringent moral or belief demands in practice, preferring prudence to scourges, since it must relate in some way to the spiritual state of nearly everyone in its community. Indeed, one can usually not uncomfortably hold skeptical thoughts within the temple, so long as one holds them privately. Many may have such an ambivalent relation to the belief of the established religion even as they participate in its rites and value the cultural and communal benefits of its tradition. At the same time, the temple will also have its devout. But from either perspective, the temple looks established in every sense, and beside it small deviant groups cannot but appear bizarre and uncouth.

Established religion is the Catholicism of Italy, the Islam of Arabia, the Buddhism of Thailand, the American Christianity of the "mainline," family-oriented Catholic and Protestant churches. On one hand, established religion merges imperceptibly into "civil religion"—on the other, into the faith of those happy ones for whom what is a deep and serious commitment happens to be no different from the faith of their fathers and what is respectable in their environment. For them the temple is all the truth they need.

The Different Ones

Others, even in the midst of temple rites, know deep down they are prisoners in the cave. In the bosom of kin and community, they feel not at home but inexpressibly different, out of harmony. Their inner sails are set to a crosswind, they are fledgling swans amid ducklings.

This sense of being spiritually "different" often starts with subjective turbulence together with acute self-consciousness; the "different" one is always, in his or her own view, more complex and aware than the rest. He or she looks out to see the same cracks in the gleaming facade of the temple as in his own soul and wonders at those still smilingly entering its portals. Perhaps, like the young Carl Jung,[2] he dreams of God defecating on a cathedral, and muses about better churches not made with hands and known only to him.

The different and more complex one may come by his difference in diverse ways—or its real source may be unknown. He may be a Greek slave in the days of the Roman Empire transported from familiar grove and shrine into one of the teeming Mediterranean cities; a Chinese of old who nodded during the stiff Confucian rites; an Englishman for whom the stately Anglican worship had only the exterior beauty of a vessel of old chased silver.

To such as these speak attractive voices, inner or outer, saying, "Come out from among them. You are ready for things they are not, and you need to show at least in a part of your life that you are not the same as they." It is a call to some other wisdom, some other initiation, which makes plain and immediate what is only dimly recognized in the official temple. It is the call of the Magus, the esoteric Taoist, the Tantrist, the Sufi, the occultist, the sectary.

The summoner's role will be that of Plato's shambler back from the light. In the West, at least, his or her allegiance is more likely than not to be to the undying Platonic and Neoplatonic spiritual tradition in some form, whether called Gnosticism, Kabbalah, Hermeticism, Theosophy, or Spiritualism.

But, also like Plato's stumbling initiate, he will doubtless appear incoherent and confused. He or she will be called an idiot or a madman or, most likely, a charlatan by the folk of the temple. Indeed, he or she may well be a combination of all these, like the shaman of yore.

Yet also like the shaman, and the light-scarred initiate, the summoner has somewhere known he or she was marked out as different from most, and can see things opaque to the multitudes. The charlatan contemptuously expresses this sense of being different in an endeavor to befuddle the others with deep words and sleight-of-hand. The mystagogue expresses the same sense in humble or proud proclamation of an alternative truth even in the face of ridicule and stones. Perhaps they are not as different as they seem. The two, in fact, often abide together in the complex personality of the spiritually different one, the right hand not knowing what the left is doing—or the right using the left to make a few technical adjustments which will help confirm the faith of others in what the wonder-worker himself deeply believes. More than most men of the temple, the returner to the cave and those drawn by his words show extremes of spiritual courage and depravity, or complex intermingling of the two.

To be sure, the American temple has known its share of people with seemingly contradictory characters. The Hawthornesque puritan whose strange inner stirrings belie his election to grace and the ambivalent Elmer Gantry evangelist are stock figures in the American imagination. Not a few successful priests and ministers combine deep commitment with passion for the power and prestige their calling can afford.

But the ambiguities of the temple are different from those of the cave in important ways. The temple is, as the religion of the community, the custodian of normative moral values, and any sacerdotal manipulation must be tacitly understood by the community to be following an acceptable style and as ultimately supportive of community values. Every community must have rights of exclusion and inclusion, of forgiveness and rejection, and of drawing the lines between them. Anyone operating within a temple structure will have a good idea what sort of behavior supports its self-image, and what does not. For every community has an idealized image, supported more by symbols and styles than concepts, of what an ideal personality is, and knows quite well what "fits" and what does not. It may be no real sin for a cleric to be ambitious, rich, or gluttonous, though he must shun drink and adultery. Or, as was almost the case in some Tantric and Taoist circles, it could be the other way around. There are kinds of crime or immorality which "fit" better in a social context than others, and so are far more easily forgiven, if the overall style of the perpetrator supports the self-image of the society. Often the wily schemer, like Jacob, Odysseus, or the trickster Coyote of Amerindian folklore, may be a beloved hero of legend whose emulators are half-admired. Or again, a cleric like Friar Tuck, self-indulgent yet lovable and warmly human, may be better liked than the moralist by many.

But the initiate from the cave seems not to fit with either the temple's virtues or its accepted vices. His ambition, unlike that of the aspirant bishop in a "mainline" church, is considered a sign of little grace; his wealth (if he has any) is held to be the gains of charlatanism, though it will probably not equal that of many established ecclesiastics in this land who live on tithes and royalties without similar imputation; his gluttony singles him out as a hypocrite, though other men of the cloth have been beloved for their girth. At the same time, he will have his devoted coterie, who do not so much defend his faults as simply not see them.

Models of Occult Conversion

The process of the individual excursus of "different ones" into a congenial group has been spelled out in more detail in Lofland and Stark's model of conversion to a non-normative religion.[3] According to them, the background factors are:

1. Perception of considerable ongoing tension, strain, deprivation, or frustration. This fits our reflections on the dissonance between the "different ones" and the establishment religion environment.

2. Possession of a "religious" rhetoric and problem-solving perspective. This implies that somewhere along the line the literature or presence of the mystagogic tradition must have reached the prospective adherent of emergent religion, who found in its teaching a way of rationalizing the tensions cited in (1).

3. Self-definition as "religious seeker." This stage involves both rejection of traditional, establishment religion, and of "secular" processes (such as psychoanalysis) as solutions to the problem.

The individual at this point would be more than ready to find his or her spiritual identity at least in part (for we must always bear in mind that many seekers are willing to carry what amounts to dual membership in both conventional established religion and emergent religion) in those options which present themselves to "seekers" rather than in what is conventional. Lofland and Stark go on to suggest further stages which result from "situational factors" in the process rather than "predisposing characteristics."

4. A turning point is reached in which old lines of action are no longer operable and contact with a "cult" member begins.

5. Development of bonds between the "pre-convert" and members of the new group begins.

6. This relationship and weakened ties with people outside the group results in "verbal conversion."

7. Finally, "total conversion" comes when interaction with the group becomes intensive and often communal, so that the new member becomes "deployable."

It should be emphasized that probably only a small percentage of seekers reach the stage of "total commitment" and availability as "deployable" agents of the new movement. Later we shall speak of the distinction between the intensive and diffuse expression of non-normative movements; the last stage of the Lofland and Stark model would clearly pertain to those who are drawn to the former.

Salient characteristics of this model, and of our own categorization of "the different ones," have been confirmed by other studies. Balch and Taylor, in their study of members of the UFO cult started in 1975 by two individuals who called themselves Bo and Peep, noted that most members were "not converts in the true sense of the word." There was not a "radical reorganization of identity." Rather, most were people who had had a consistent record as "different ones." It was the last stage in the process of people who had been for a long time protean in life-style, alienated, and involved in cults, communes, self-actualization techniques, and esoteric world views. This group was not, then, a radically new identity—but the decision to join it was a "*reaffirmation* of their seekership." Most had been in such groups before, and most were able to rationalize in advance the possibility of disillusionment by saying that "the Two" were not important in themselves, but the whole episode would just be another opportunity to "grow," even if it turned out to be a hoax. This attitude maintains a confirmed population of "different ones" and enables them to live with the charlatanism that sometimes seeks them out, and even to "grow" according to their own esoteric lights despite, or through, the shadow side of their esoteric world.[4] Other studies have shown that people who value the eclectic inner quest are likely to be better educated and more intellectually sophisticated than the average, and perhaps they are able in their own way to sort these things out.

The paradigm suggested by these writers has been reinforced by Frederick R. Lynch's study of adherents of a group he calls the Church of the Sun.[5] He has divided the process of conversion and commitment into four phases. The first consists of intellectual curiosity and individual reading in occult and mystical literature; we can presuppose behind this interest some long-standing degree of alienation and sense of being "different" that the seeker is attempting to interpret. The second stage is more subjective; its elements may be emotional conviction, personal psychic and mystical experiences, together with tension and stress. In the third stage, the preconvert meets a charismatic occultist and/or visits a congenial occult group. Finally he adheres to it to receive social support, even as he senses individual growth and development.

Metaphors for Established and Emergent Religion

Our issue is not to assess the relative virtues and vices of establishment and emergent religionists, but to understand why it is that they are perceived, and perceive themselves, in different ways, even when they do or say fundamentally the same things. It is clearly a matter of differing roles within the society, which amounts to a matter of perception. The initiate is perceived, by both his detractors and supporters, as a novelty and the bearer of novelty. To his foes he is a dangerous disturber of a stable and tranquil social order; to his enthusiasts a light-bringer of a new age. L. Ron Hubbard has been attacked as the founder of the "dangerous new cult of Scientology" and labeled as he who "wears the boots of responsibility for this universe" by himself and his followers.

But claims comparable to this have been made in America for a long time. One thinks of Jemima Wilkinson, the "Publick Universal Friend" of early nineteenth-century upstate New York, Mother Ann Lee of the Shakers, John Noyes of the Oneida Community, or

Thomas Lake Harris of Fountain Grove. These people and their movements were considered, like Scientology or the "Hare Krishnas" of today, "new and different," as though these terms were synonymous.

Yet the very existence of the nineteenth-century predecessors, and even before, suggests that the different is not always new in form or social role. Instead it may be a part of an ongoing pattern of alternative spirituality. Just as we have not always recognized what the study of Balch and Taylor showed—that most converts to new, non-normative groups are likely to have been in several similar groups before, and are not really converts in the sense of making a radical change in self-identity and life-style—so we have not always recognized that the whole non-normative religious world is not as new or alien as it seems. What underlies these conceptions, or misconceptions, is the operative basic conceptual metaphor for religion, that which plays the role of what Stephen C. Pepper has called a "root metaphor."[6]

We often think of the sociological expression of religion as taking two forms. In the Troeltschian tradition, these are commonly called "church" and "sect," or "church" and "withdrawal groups," the latter broken down into "sects" and "cults." As indicated, I prefer the terms "established" and "emergent" religion. Established religion is that which is, like the "temple," culturally and institutionally pervasive in the society, and which is also assimilated by folk culture and embodied in many of its motifs.

The dictionary meanings of the word "emergent" are several, all of which suggest characteristics of a contrasting manifestation of religion: emerging out of a fluid that covers or conceals; arising suddenly and unexpectedly; arising as a natural or logical consequence of a prior event; appearing as or involving the appearance of something novel or in a process of evolution; and, as a noun, a plant visible above others, as a tree much higher than the level of the forest. A quality of emergence suggested by several of these definitions is that the absolute novelty of its appearance is deceptive; it is something that was there all the time or is fully understandable in terms of known logic or processes. But the emergent form was concealed; it did not or does not become visible until certain changes in the total environment occur, or a certain angle of perception is achieved. When this happens it is likely to strike one as a novelty, as something vastly different and amazing.

An emergent religion, then, is one which appears suddenly and unexpectedly, and which stands out from the sea of established religion like a new volcanic island or a rock revealed by an unusually low tide. Though it may be a result of an understandable process and even something which in a sense was there all along, it gives an appearance of both novelty and striking contrast to the established faiths that surround it.

Let us return to the matter of root metaphors and see in what way they contribute to this perception. What conceptual metaphors do we commonly and half-consciously use to understand the role of established religion? I would like to suggest they are geological. We think of the established religion, or what we conceive to be the established religion, of a society as coterminous with entities like "culture" and "society," which we then imagine as static, underlying substrata out of which individual lives, and more ephemeral social movements, arise and decline like grass or summer flowers. Under the influence of ideas like Comte's distinction between "social statics" and "social dynamics," we think of established religion and what goes with it as unchanging ground—like the See of Peter, a rock. We may even think of it, like "culture," as comprised of several geological layers: the bedrock of "folk religion," the loam of institutionalism, the topsoil of the intellectual "great tradition." But short of earthquakes, all are as unmoving in relation to the span of ordinary lives as the earth upon which our cities and temples are built; they slide only inches per century.

In the late twentieth century, it should hardly be necessary to spell out the inadequacies of this metaphor. While the distinction between established and emergent religion has not been erased, we have seen that the conceptualization of the former as static and coextensive with "ground" entities like "culture" and "society" does not fit the facts. Institutions as paradigmatic of established religion as the Roman Catholic Church, the Confucian tradition in China, or traditional religions in Africa have undergone rapid change or been toppled from primacy within their spheres of influence. Whatever the contrast between established and emergent religion, it is not between that which changes and that which changes not, or at a slower rate—the former can change at a rate which parallels the rise and fall of new spiritual movements when conditions are right. Moreover, established religion is not necessarily coextensive with "culture" or "society"—a dominant church certainly will affect different people or groups to very different extents, and may touch important segments of the population very little, yet still be the most important religion of the society in the sense of holding the "established" heritage.

More important, the past was not as different in these respects as the static view of established religion and culture indicates. To be sure, there are those who will hold that the twentieth century is a time of unprecedentedly rapid and drastic change, when cultures which *were* geologically static for millennia have been bulldozed into the harsh light of modernity. Undoubtedly modern change has important special characteristics and can be seen in significant respects as a unique global transition. But its uniqueness can be, and often is, misleadingly wedded to another conceptual paradigm, one which has been common coin of prophets and social commentators from ancient Greece and Israel to the present: the past as a kind of timeless mythic *illud tempus* when people lived more quietly and were more religious than now, against which a present of change and, usually, fall from grace, can be showcased. This reading of the history of religion is hardly valid. As Paul Radin has shown, primitive societies have their share of skeptics and of the irreligious just as do modern societies.[9] The Middle Ages were hardly a static "Age of Faith" on either the inner or outer planes, except, for different reasons, in the eyes of Whig and Catholic romantic historians. Few significant societies have long endured without political and spiritual turmoil engendered by intercultural confrontation.

In contrast to the geological metaphor of established religion, under what metaphorical umbrella do we commonly contemplate emergent religion? It is, I think, biological. Victor Turner, referring to the work of Robert A. Nisbet, has underscored the significance in the social sciences of metaphors of "growth" and "development," and, conversely, of the "sickness," "decay," and even "death" of societies.[10] It should be obvious that this metaphorical language makes the observer aware of certain phenomena, but may well obscure his perception of others. As in grand Hegelian and Marxian schemas, or dispensationalism, the significance of the small but, arguably, only real historical units, microevents and individual lives, is likely to be collapsed into the significance of where they fall in the process.

The grand conceptualizations of history rooted in the biological and evolutionary metaphors of Hegel, Marx, Spengler, or Toynbee, are (except for the second) not in high favor at the moment. But in the study of emergent religion they are still with us. We tend to think of a "new religious movement" in terms of a beginning, a process of development or unfolding, moments of crisis and transition, periods of maturity, and finally perhaps decay and death. This metaphor has been assisted by the popular use of Weberian categories for understanding new movements: the Weberian prophet or mystagogue is the "founder"—the "seed," one might say—of the movement; the "routinization of charisma" process in the movement's second generation seems clearly to legitimize thinking in developmental terms.

Of course, all of these categories are valid; they all have reference to real observations which have been confirmed time and again. But let us reflect on what might be hidden, as well as what is revealed, by a fundamental set of "root metaphors" for religion which picture established religion as layers of "geological" substrata virtually coextensive with culture or society, and new, non-normative religious movements as "biological" growths which rise out of them and finally collapse back into them as they decay.

Metaphors of Coexistence

Suppose we were to think instead of metaphors like the ones suggested by our discussion of emergence: the sea, and the rock always beneath it but only occasionally revealed; the forest in which from certain perspectives a tree stands out against the skyline. What we are getting at, of course, is a dualistic rather than a process metaphor. We are thinking of what we have called the temple and the cave, the Methodist and the Spiritualist churches, "mainline" religion and what is commonly (though, if our metaphor were to be adopted, misleadingly) associated with "cult" or "new" religions.

Suppose we were to think of these pairs of categories as representing two modes of religious experience and behavior that conformed equally to aspects of human subjectivity, were equally long-lasting, and were also equally susceptible to change. The chief difference would be that the "temple" sort tends to take expression in the established manner, and the "cave" sort in the emergent. The latter, particularly in the context of American culture, fulfills an attribute of its intrinsic nature by rising and falling, coming and going, from the line of sight of the temple porch. As a true opposite, it is the reverse of those values by which the temple is comprehended. It lacks conspicuous institutional continuity, is represented more by a series of charismatic than routinized leaders, and exalts the unstable-seeming initiate from the cave rather than one who is able to handle the affairs of a society's normative values.

But the "two sides" metaphor—no more "true" than the biological one—brings in some important points about this elusive and reverse tradition. First, it gives conceptual priority to the tradition itself, rather than to the rise and fall of individual personalities and movements within it. Second, it reminds us that the tradition has a history of its own and does not begin anew with every new outcropping of it. Third, it shows us that the two sides are in continual interface and interaction, not least within individuals themselves. Fourth, it keeps in mind that the alternative tradition is an opposite, and that much of what is true about its structure, meaning, and work can only be rightly understood by turning upside down the criteria that we apply to the temple.

We think, for example, of temple institutions as being huge and solid, and those of the other side—like the Spiritualist church—as being ephemeral and almost microscopic. In a sense, they are. Spiritualist churches come and go with the popularity of various mediums, who even buy and sell them. The Spiritualist church described earlier in this chapter was founded under its present name only in 1969 or thereabouts, and the minister who endeavored to make it the flagship of a new Spiritualist denomination has already left for another state. Yet the point is that new Spiritualist churches, and other even more important manifestations of the emergent wing of American religion, keep appearing even as others decline. Comparing them to the mighty "church" of Troeltschean sociology, is like comparing the amoeba to the whale—they are tiny, short-lived, continuously dividing, yet in one sense far more immortal.

The Significance of the Metaphor

Certainly a metaphor like this sets up two "ideal types," and such images very easily lead to serious misconceptions, not least in appreciation of interaction. As I shall argue more fully later on, the metaphor's significance is not chiefly in the realm of social expressions of religion. If one were to label all churches in America as temple or cave, the result would be misleading both statistically, for the two have differing relations to that kind of expression, and inferentially, for the relationship between them is such that many groups would have characteristics of both. In fact, as we shall see, the real divide is not in history or sociology, but within the individual and social psyches of Americans—and here (not in sociology) the dualism of the model has some ineluctable significance, since it is related to the basic binary patterns of human thought.

But it might be well to explore further the sociological values of the dualistic metaphor. A good example of the other approach might be found in J. Milton Yinger's monumental work in the Troeltschean tradition of sociology of religion, *Religion, Society, and the Individual.*[11] The sort of religion we are concerned with is what here finds its structural expression in the "cult," an entity at the opposite end of the scale from the Universal Church, the Ecclesia, or even the Denomination. It is characterized as being of small size and short life, centered around the charismatic leader, having beliefs at great variance with those of the community, basically concerned with mystical experience and personal problems. They are, and significantly a biological term is used, religious "mutants." Spiritualism is cited as illustrative of cult religion.

G. K. Nelson, in his admirable study of Spiritualism, argues that Yinger's characterization does not do justice to it. Far from being short-lived, some Spiritualist institutions have survived over a century, while admittedly perpetuating a religion at great variance with community beliefs, and centered on "mystical" experience and personal problems. More important, even though the great majority of Spiritualist institutions come and go, the movement seems able to replenish itself without benefit of the kind of educational facilities and institutional solidity which undergirds "mainline" churches.[12] It seems, in other words, to play by different rules.

Our model, on the other hand, would emphasize and give a conceptual framework for the continuities of Spiritualism—as well as (to name only the three traditions discussed at length in this book) the relationship of Theosophy with Spiritualism and of American Zen to Theosophy. It would underscore a metaphorical reading of each individual movement, or personal experience, of the "cave" sort as only an epiphenomenon of a vaster presence which is, in its way, as puissant and lasting as the temple. But it is different, and works by different laws. Its strengths and weaknesses are, in fact, the opposing complement to those of the temple: it has protean flexibility where the latter has visible continuing structure; it has appeal to subjectivity as established religion evokes one's sense of family and community and place, as it continually changes, divides, regroups.

As James T. Richardson has pointed out, a cult—and one could add the emergent spiritual tradition as a whole—has as its major criterion its "oppositional" character.[13] Its beliefs and practices both are counter to those of the dominant culture, or when that culture is in a state of dissolution, to those of other subcultural groups. In fact, this opposition is not only in belief and practice, but in the entire "style" of being religious informed by a very different sociological experience which nonetheless has its own continuities. We thus affirm the main thrust of the "structuralist" argument of Roy Wallis, that "cults" are distinguished by certain structural features much at variance with normative churches. Wallis mentions individualism, eclecticism, and a "fragile" character which is often focussed on a charismatic leader; "cults," in his view, are not distinguished by any particular doctrine, but by symbols of opposition to social norms.[14]

But one can also agree with Richardson that ideological content is an important symbol of this opposition. I would further argue, without minimizing the structuralist aspect of a definition of "cult," that ideology and structure in any social movement are usually profoundly if subtly intertwined on the "deep structure" level, so that certain types of ideology tend to bring forth certain structures, and vice versa.

In European and American culture, at least, there is an ongoing "cultic milieu" or "emergent religion" tradition to which new "cult" or "excursus" movements almost inevitably relate themselves, and from which they draw, to reify their oppositional stance, style and substance. However different on the surface in content, and however new a revelation they claim, this tradition often provides implicit models for the structure and ideology of a new-formed excursus oppositional group, and usually an implicit validation of its existence.

Our model far better fits the self-conception of alternative groups than does the biological, for if anything unites the subjective experiences of these groups, it is conviction that what they are participating in is not rightly understood by emphasizing the smallness, recentness, and marginality of the group. They may have explanations both metaphysical and sociological for that, and individuals may understand the relation between their own sense of "differentness" and the appeal of a minority group. But they will also insist that their group is older and deeper than the more visible churches. Thus Spiritualism, not unaware of its parallels with paleolithic shamanism, calls itself "the oldest religion in the world." Theosophy speaks of its lore as "the Ancient Wisdom." Zen claims to be the essential but unspoken message of the Buddha, if not something even older than the Enlightened One. However one chooses to evaluate these claims, a hermeneutical method which does not obstruct phenomenological empathy with the self-understanding of the religion under study is desirable. More than developmentalism, this method may, in fact, offer a crucial clue to understanding not only their inner life, but their place in American society.

2 *Excursus Religion*

Visits to the Other Shore

If emergent religion is the alternative to which those who turn away from established religion of the temple have recourse, their journeys are individual excursions. If the emergent religious tradition has certain unifying themes, and a hidden history which shows continuities among its many manifestations past and present, for each voyager the journey is unique and solitary because it enacts a personal subjective quest. However much both goal and pilgrim path may pre-exist or conform to well-trodden patterns, the experience ordinarily comes to a person conditioned by normative cultural religion as an excursus away from the familiar and toward that which draws just because it is strange, yet in its very strangeness seems to offer a promise of new kinds of self-discovery.

In 1809, speaking at Nurnberg on educational theory, G. W. F. Hegel made these remarks:

> Inherent in the strange and remote is a powerful interest, . . . the attractiveness of which is in inverse proportion to its familiarity . . .
> Initially it is in this remoteness that depth must be sought; this is a necessary seeking for illusion. But the depth and strength which we attain can be measured only by the distance to which we have fled from the familiar center in which we first found ourselves embedded, and to which we strive to return. From this centrifugal impetus of the soul derives its compulsion to achieve for itself the desired separation from its natural essence and condition . . . . But that which separates us from ourselves contains at the same time all the starting-points and threads of the return to ourselves, of its inner affinity, and of the rediscovery of ourselves, but now finally of ourselves according to the true and general essence of the spirit.[1]

W. R. Irwin has spoken of this individual Hegelian process—when for the subject even the owl of Minerva nods to dream, or, becoming distracted, tarries in her flight down the centuries—as "the excursion and return of the soul."[2] Minerva's human servitors then turn aside from the idea whose time has come, whether nineteenth-century Western triumphalism or the alleged secularity of the twentieth century, to savor something else.

The religious quest that leads away from the ordinary and established religion could be called an excursus—and, collectively, excursus religion. Its opposite might be termed familiar religion, with a certain emphasis on the origin of the word in *familia*, for it is intertwined with the ethnic and community structures communicated to one through family. Excursus religion, then, is individual or group participation in what on a large scale is emergent religion.

For the excursus of any individual or small group is likely to lead soon or late to the enchanted forest of the enduring, if often hidden, pattern of emergent religion. That is because the singularity of the quest seeks completion in identification with a tradition, however arcane; both the vast but invisible cloud of witnesses and the loneliness of the initiate in this world help define his experience. A society, therefore, will have not only its stock symbols of identity with the social structures, but also its stock symbols of alienation. As we shall see, in America such symbols as meditation, monism, feminine spiritual leadership, and orientation toward a distant and exotic culture have been among those signaling an excursus toward the emergent shore. Often the humor of a culture reveals better than more formal statements its stock symbols of alienation and excursus; in American wit about religion, the long tradition of jokes featuring wild-eyed sandaled men preaching imminent doom and bemused middle-aged matrons gushing over soulful-eyed swamis bears them ungrateful testimony.

Excursus religion is a spiritual movement away from ordinary social and psychic structures alike, for a quest will steadily reassemble both as they impinge upon consciousness to mirror each other. Excursus religion can be discussed from both social scientific and psychological perspectives, and nothing about it is more instructive than its revelations concerning the profound interaction of these two spheres of human operation. But let us first, in this chapter, emphasize the social scientific approach in American historical perspective.

Grid and Group in America

I would like to start by attempting a brief application of certain categories of the anthropologist Mary Douglas to the American religious situation. There is a place in this model for non-normative cultic religion which reveals, I believe, some significant facts about it and its role in American spirituality. Douglas's fundamental hypothesis is that cosmological theories have their roots in social experience.[3] While this is by no means a new idea, she provides a novel and very stimulating model for the correlation of cosmologies and societies. The model rests on the assumption that humans desire consonance at all levels of experience; the same style and texture is sought in subjective, intrahuman, and transcendent relationships.

Douglas's model consists of two basic variables, "grid" and "group." Grid refers to the systems, classifications, and symbols by which one brings order to experience, and so to society and to the cosmos. A social example of grid in practice is caste in India. Group refers to social pressure and indicates the degree to which the group establishes its boundaries and constrains its members' identities. It indicates the extent to which one's place in the caste system inescapably shapes the contours of life. Every society has both grid and group forces, but their relative strengths vary considerably, producing not only very different types of human social life, but very different types of religious symbols to articulate it and views of divinity and transcendence to validate it. Particularly significant clues lie in the society's attitudes toward the meaning of sin and the cause of suffering; toward the roles of trance, magic, and ritual; toward purity and pollution; and toward the meaning of personal identity. Let us examine attitudes relevant to religion which pertain to each of the four kinds of social organization the model yields.

Here are the categories and relevant attitudes as summarized by Sheldon R. Isenberg and Dennis E. Owen.[4] It is important to note that each set begins with the attitude toward purity. Then, working through the attitude toward the closely related ritual and magic categories, and through attitudes toward identity and the two aspects of self-hood (body and the powers of mind—trance or meditation), finally reaches the interface of self and the transcendent in the category of sin. It projects the whole system in a cosmology and a cosmic view of suffering and misfortune.

Strong Group and Grid

Purity: strong concern for purity; well-defined purification rituals; purity rules define and maintain social structure

Ritual: a ritualistic society; ritual expresses the internal classification system

Magic: belief in the efficacy of symbolic behavior

Personal Identity: a matter of internalizing clearly articulated social roles; individual subservient to but not in conflict with society

Body: tightly controlled but a symbol of life

Trance: dangerous; either not allowed or tightly controlled and limited to a group of experts

Sin: the violation of formal rules; focus on behavior instead of internal state of being; ritual (magic) efficacious in counteracting sin

Cosmology: anthropomorphic, nondualistic, the universe is just and noncapricious

Suffering and Misfortune: the result of automatic punishment for the violation of formal rules; part of the divine economy

Strong Group, Weak Grid

Purity: strong concern for purity but the inside of the social and physical bodies are under attack; pollution present and purification ritual ineffective

Ritual: ritualistic; ritual focused upon group boundaries, concerned with expelling pollutants (witches) from social body

Magic: ineffective in protecting individual and social bodies; a source of danger and pollution

Personal Identity: located in group membership, not in the internalization of roles, which are confused; distinction between appearance and internal state

Body: social and physical bodies tightly controlled but under attack; invaders have broken through bodily boundaries; not a symbol of life

Trance: dangerous; a matter of demonic possession; evil

Sin: a matter of pollution; evil lodged within person and society; sin much like a disease; internal state of being more important than adherence to formal rules, but the latter still valued

Cosmology: anthropomorphic; dualistic; warring forces of good and evil; universe is not just and may be whimsical

Suffering and Misfortune: unjust; not automatic punishment; attributed to malevolent forces

Weak Group, Strong Grid

Purity: pragmatic attitude; pollution not automatic; bodily waste not threatening, may be recycled

Ritual: will be used for private ends if present; ego remains superior; condensed symbols do not delimit reality

Magic: private; may be a strategy for success

Personal Identity: pragmatic and adaptable

Body: instrumental; self-controlled; pragmatic attitude

Trance: not dangerous

Sin: failure; loss of face; stupidity

Cosmology: geared to individual success and initiative; cosmos is benignly amoral; God as junior partner

Suffering and Misfortune: an intelligent person ought to be able to avoid them

Weak Group, Weak Grid

Purity: rejected; anti-purity

Ritual: rejected; anti-ritual; effervescent; spontaneity valued

Magic: none; magic rejected

Personal Identity: no antagonism between society and self but old society may be seen as oppressive; roles rejected, self-control and social control low

Body: irrelevant; life is spiritual; purity concerns absent but body may be rejected; may be used freely or asceticism may prevail

Trance: approved, even welcomed; no fear of loss of self-control
Sin: a matter of ethics and interiority
Cosmology: likely to be impersonal; individual access, usually direct; no mediation; benign
Suffering and Misfortune: love conquers all

I would like to propose that American society in the young Republic was, as a whole, one of weak group and grid. This was especially true on the frontier and more a matter of expansive American self-perception and Jeffersonian-Jacksonian idealism than of fact. Very strong grid and group patterns remained in some subcultures, particularly with regard to slavery and social class. But self-perceptions are important, and certainly the general ethos of the new nation reflected a combination of enlightenment rationalist rejection of ritual and magic, a deistic impersonalizing and democratizing of the cosmos, and the frontier's freedom from oppressive social roles and social control.

Against the almost oppressive vacuity of weak group and grid, however, arose certain reactions. Clearly, the fundamentalist-evangelical religion of past and present grounded in the great revivals exemplifies strong group, weak grid characteristics. The crucial importance this tradition places on establishing a boundary between the circle of purity and pollution (that is, between the "saved" and the "world") but through group membership and internal state rather than through ritual or formal roles, and its corresponding insistence on distinction between appearance and internal state, bears that out. So does the tradition's well-known and sometimes almost obsessive mistrust of anything that smacks of ritual, magic, trance, meditation, or "the occult," and the vociferousness with which polluting persons, things, or ideas are often shunned or cast out. Finally, one sees the cosmological consequence of fundamentalism and evangelicalism in its anthropomorphic and dualistic theology, and not least in its sometimes lively sense of demonic intervention in the affairs of humankind. In the revival situation, of course, both the group pressure, which is its dynamic, and the construction of the alternative world of its cosmology and perception of personal identity are intensified to the utmost.

Another American spiritual tradition which has probably equaled evangelicalism's influence is the cult of optimism and success based on belief in the power of mind and attitude to transcend problems. This is the tradition which, rooted in transcendentalism, appears in "New Thought," Christian Science, and, more recently, "positive thinking" and many comparable quasi-religious, quasi-psychological teachings about the "science" of constructive thought. This tradition (excluding the strong group aspect of Christian Science) has many characteristics in common with the weak group, strong grid pattern. Perhaps that is because of its sociological background in the primordial American weak group ambience joined with the implicit status-consciousness of the later successful capitalists who have been its most typical adherents. One finds in the literature of this tradition a basically pragmatic attitude in which failure is the real sin, in which all sorts of semi-rituals and semi-magic may be used as a means of strengthening the positive thoughts which are the forces through which the ego attains success. The cosmology generally amounts to a benign monism in which meditative trance is not inappropriate (for there is a mystical and "metaphysical" cast to the theology), and in which many wells of power may be tapped by the one who has both initiative and adaptability.

Now we come to the kind of religion which is the topic of this study, the "non-normative" religion more strikingly discontinuous with the cultural background than the above and attained by excursus. My hypothesis is that its basic characteristics are those of strong group and grid. However, some of these characteristics need to be translated to understand their application to a tiny dissident group, instead of a vast society like traditional China or India. Moreover, it needs to be understood—and this is a point to which we shall return later—that strong grid and group represent an ideal which compels, in the spirit of Hegel's attractiveness of the strange and opposite, just because it *is* the most direct antipode of the basic American weak grid and group. It is an ideal, however, which can only be completed symbolically, and in the relating of present excursus religious life to paradigmatic histories and cosmologies overflowing with tokens of invisible but very real strong grids and groups to which the initiate belongs. Excursus is the spirituality of fascination with symbols of strong grid and group.

Thus, even when the group is small and ephemeral, its leadership is likely to have fairly unusual and imposing titles, suggesting continuity with ancient mystery schools, churches of the apostolic succession, or lineages of Eastern gurus or masters, and to stress that authentication. The cosmology is likely to feature a nondualist Absolute rather than a personal God, and sin is a violation of rules which is punished automatically by karma, thus fulfilling the rule of order on the metaphysical plane. But between the Absolute and the more chaotic world here below there is likely to range a vast but ordered hierarchy of intermediate masters, spirits, polytheistic gods, or kabbalistic spheres. This pleroma suggests at once the order and compulsion of a vast strong grid and group assembly to which one is privy, and the reality of numinous but anthropomorphic beings with whom one can have a warmer relation than to the impersonal Absolute. It is one's place as a novice in this hierarchy that one internalizes, as well as whatever place one may have in the sociological order, even though that role might bring one into conflict with empirical society.

The group's putative history serves a comparable function. At the end of the last chapter, we alluded to the tendency of religions in the emergent tradition to see themselves as older than more normative churches, whatever the appearances. Continuity with shamanism or the ancient mysteries provides a strong grid and group dimension in time, as does rapport with invisible hierarchies in space—or perhaps one should say hyperspace.

As we observed in connection with the cave metaphor, initiation has a definite place in a strong grid and group spiritual world. Its characteristic concern for purity is evidenced in concern for initiation (for initiation is purification), although it may also be expressed in such practices as vegetarianism and the formation of communes where strong grid and group can be reified.

Although excursus religion may be as ritualistic and magical as a ceremonial magic order, or as unritualistic as a theosophical lodge which offers little more than lectures, a sense of the importance of symbol and symbolic behavior pervades nearly all of it. There may be, however, some inconsistency in the matter of trance, for according to our model it is considered "dangerous" and "either not allowed or tightly controlled and limited to a group of experts" in strong grid and group social organization. The great importance of meditation, mediumistic trance, and the like in American excursus religion seems at odds with this criterion. Perhaps so. Yet the need for skill and authenticity in the practice of meditation is, in fact, the chief reason for existence of a number of important groups. Organizations like Zen centers, the Maharishi Mahesh Yogi's Transcendental Meditation movement, yoga centers, the Divine Light Mission, and many others certainly wish to promote wide-spread use of meditation. Yet the fact that they offer legitimated teachers of it who are often members of a long lineage of such teachers indicates it should be taught only by experts, and implies it is useless or dangerous when it is not. Such control has also been one rationale for the formation of Spiritualist denominations, as weak as they have been. Thus, although the widespread use of meditation has been an important symbol of differentiation from other segments of American religion, and although the enhance-ment of subjectivity it allows is very important to the psychology of excursus religion, it has not escaped equally energetic constraints.

Cosmic and metahistorical strong grid and group, then, con-structs a heavenly city of purity, order, and identity in which the man or woman of excursus devoutly wishes to dwell. We must now consider further the way to it and the signs of its appearing.

Liminality and Communitas

As Isenberg and Owen suggest, the work of Victor Turner offers models which complement and extend the insights of Mary Doug-las very nicely.[5] What we are concerned with is the appeal of one grid and group arrangement in the context of another, and this means understanding alienation, initiation, and the appeal of an alternative reality. An important area of Turner's work has been the analysis of initiatory passage and the enactment of social ideals.

In *The Ritual Process*,[6] Turner explores the three steps of ini-tiation defined in Gerardus van Gennep's classic study of initiation, *The Rites of Passage*. These are (1) the separation of the candidate out from his group, (2) margin or limen, and (3) reaggregation or reincorporation of the initiate as a member of a new group, or of the old group with a new status.

Of these the middle stage, liminality, is doubtless the most mysterious. It is the status of the novice during his time in the initiatory lodge, tomorrow's knight at his nocturnal vigil before the altar, the future king being jousted and jeered by his prospective subjects. It is a time of the reversal of all customary structures and restraints. The subject is ritually naked and downcast, betwixt and between. But since at the same time this state negates all the restrictions of structure, in a paradoxical way it is an opening of the doors of infinity, akin to that mystical experience which also requires a stripping away of all worldly garb. These two sides, degradation and the plenitude of a *coincidentia oppositorum,* are well expressed in the language which compares liminal states to death, the womb, invisibility, bisexuality, and journeys in the wilderness.

Liminality is originally a process state, a state of transition. But for some—especially when the quest seems endless—it can become a permanent state, a continual calling. This is the meaning of monks and holy wanderers of all sorts, who manifest it to themselves and to the world through special garb and a reversal of ordinary usage in the matters of sex, family, money, authority, and habitation. They symbolize to the community that an opposite of the "natural" is a possible human ideal, that structure can be transcended, or, rather, replaced with an antipodal structure. Liminality, perhaps inspired by the ideal of the monk, is also a quadrant on the inner compass of many who do not wear it as a robe; they are like the people of the cave paradigm.

Understanding liminality is clearly very important to understanding excursus religion, for it is into the sea of liminality that the latter ventures. Yet it is not a journey without charts, for in emergent religion ways of negotiating liminality can be made traditional, as they are in numerous ordinary religious settings. Certain people and social organizations embody and institutionalize liminality: they are able to do so because liminality usually both breaks structure and is provided for by the social structure in approved contexts. Nothing is more basic to Hindu society than recognition that to become a sadhu is the acknowledged and honorable way to move out of the structure of caste obligations. In America, excursus religion is what might be called "established means" of touching the liminality borne by such avatars of otherness as spirit mediums and Zen masters.

But even if such groups and people provide institutionalized and legitimatized glimpses into another world beyond that of the primary structures, as do all groups which participate in Frederick Streng's definition of religion as "means of ultimate transformation."[7] they do point to something beyond, of which persons, groups, and symbols are only images. That, according to Victor Turner, is the ideal of a social or perhaps eschatological state which transcends structure. In this state individuals are related in the "I-thou" manner rather than through roles. Reactions are spontaneous. It is the goal, we are told, of utopias and countercultures, and it is adumbrated in festivals and pilgrimages. Turner calls this state communitas.

Can the desire for unstructured communitas correlate with the excursus quest for plenitude of grid and group? I believe that it can, and, indeed, that in this quest strong grid and group are intended as symbols of communitas. In a traditionally strong grid and group society, the search for communitas might take other forms. But in America, strong grid and group is intended to articulate a sense of infinite but unimpeded relationships extended to every corner of space and time—in the words of the title of one famous Spiritualist book, an "unobstructed universe." It is actually structure, a plenitude of group and grid structure, which makes this possible, for the lines of its sinews are lines of communication, whereas for the excursus mind, lack of structure implies a chaos in which no real transcendent (or interhuman) communication or relationship is possible. The sense of meaningful roles in the context of ultimate reality and infinite dimensions arises from seeing oneself as a part of the unending hierarchy of heaven and earth—whether of spirits, masters, or buddhas—and is protected by strong grid and group symbols.

Mary Douglas herself seems to miss this point when she says, "No one would deliberately choose the elaborated code and the personal control system who is aware of the seeds of alienation it contains."[8] There are those for whom the lack of code and control seems far more alienating, and their presence—especially when chiefly reified as an internal symbol system relating one to cosmic transcendence—is far more a preservative of place and so of "standing" before the universe. As Isenberg and Owens posit, when we

seek relationships unmediated by roles—Turner's pure communitas
—we find that the very intimacy we sought is foreclosed, for
intimacy requires communication, and communication requires
structure.[9] Language itself is structure and is symbiotic with the
general structures of thought and society. These last—insofar as the
self is a social construct, exemplified by acquisition of language and
internalization of family and social place—are requisite to there
being anyone capable of sharing intimacy or seeking communitas.

Indeed, those occasions which best embody communitas—the
festival (and even orgy), pilgrimage, utopian societies—are in practice bound to have a structure, often a very strong structure, precisely to facilitate the new social and cosmic intimacy they incarnate.
As we have suggested in the case of the monk, the outsider's
liminal state is represented far more by symbols of reversal of the
ordinary structures than by any absolute transcendence of the realm
of symbol.

The same is suggested by the lives of those who, like the UFO
cultists mentioned in the last chapter, progress by endeavoring to
"grow" from one facet to another of the "cultic milieu." Each
"experience" is itself a symbol, as is the life-pattern as a whole—
with its "oppositional" or reversal relationship to the dominant
culture a major message. But the particular experiences, at their
fullest, may indeed be experiences of liminality. Liminality is that
breaking of structure which, through its own symbols and experiences, adumbrates communitas. It is about as far as we actually get
in this sublunar world, for communitas like Streng's "ultimate
transformation" cannot be completed among humans as we are
without paradox, and like the Buddhist nirvana cannot be concep-
tualized as attained, but is only as an awakening symbol in the
mind.

We shall find, then, that the processes of excursus religion
actually follow models like the initiation model analyzed by van
Gennep and Turner. Individuals drawn to excursus religion first
undergo a detachment from ordinary society. Frederick Evans,
Madame Blavatsky, and Jack Kerouac first left home for a period of
extensive wandering, and societies like the Shakers and Theosophists were groups of people with little sense of direction but a
definite sense of separation before they coalesced into counter-

societies. Then there is the liminal state, a state of deep initiatory separation when the transcendent and communitas reality seems close and the ordinary social realities seem unreal. This is exemplified by the early days of the Shakers under Mother Ann Lee, the Theosophists on the journey to India to be later described, the Zen year described in *The Dharma Bums*. Thirdly, the period of reaggregation comes. This is not, however, a simple reabsorption into the prior social order, any more than the initiate becomes just what he was before. Rather, it is a rationalization of the life of the group, or of the incorporated member, into its own symbol-of-reversal structures that allow it to continue both distinctive from surrounding society and yet placed within it. Here it is that symbols of the ongoing emergent religion tradition are likely to become prominent (the Spiritualism of the Shakers), and also that strong grid and group symbols move firmly into place. (The nascent excursus religion is likely to show some characteristics of strong group and weak grid.)

Excursus religion, then, is likely to manifest strong grid and group internal symbols and structures, which demarcate it from the basal weak grid and group of American society, and the strong group or grid only of evangelicalism and positive thinking. These symbols and structures are partly drawn from the treasures of the long-standing emergent religion tradition and are partly internal or putative. There are, however, definite forms which the visible tip of its expression are likely to take.

Excursus Religion and the Forms of Religious Expression

Let us examine excursus religion in terms of the three forms of religious expression proposed by the sociologist of religion Joachim Wach.[10] These are: the *theoretical*, the religion's conceptual and verbal expression in philosophy, doctrine, and myth; the *practical*, the religion's praxis in worship, rite, prayer, pilgrimage, and so forth; and the *sociological*, the styles of group, leadership, and interpersonal relations the religion indicates. In all these areas, we shall find the excursus experience generates its own symbols.

A common characteristic of excursus religion in all forms of expression is this: despite its overall oppositional stance, it seeks to

find some niche in which it is not directly competitive with normative religion. It does not set up altar against altar, or doctrine
against doctrine, in opposition to the Judeo-Christian establishment, so much as present itself as dealing with aspects of life other
than established religion, and with teachings which, rightly understood, only complement the received confessions. These movements are ostensibly noncompetitive with the great denominations,
even as they survive on religious interests and needs aroused—but
perhaps not met—by them.

This characteristic is most apparent in the sociology of excursus
religion, and it is this form of expression we shall consider first.
Sociologically, emergent and excursus religion avoids being directly
competitive with established religion by taking either more diffuse
or more intensive forms than the normative. Instead of the network
of institutionalized churches of the standard denomination, it will
have intensive centers which approach being total institutions, as
well as other forms of private participation or interest in the spiritual path which are not seen as competitive with normative religion. Thus, as we shall see, excursus religion is capable of the
intense community and full-time practice of a Shaker community, a
Zen center, or the life of a Blavatsky and an Olcott during and after
their journey to India.

This manner of life approaches that of what Erving Goffman
would call a "total institution": comparable to existence in a
prison, insane asylum, royal court, boarding school, or monastery,
it determines nearly all of one's behavior, all one's expression of
identity.[11] The horarium from dawn to dusk, the manner of eating
and sleeping, the dress and speech and, presumably, one's thoughts
and prayers—all are controlled. At its epicenters excursus religion is
dotted with such "asylums." They are not necessarily permanent
residences, for many come and many go. As Hegel realized, the
"Other" has a strong attraction, but there is also a strong undertow
to return, for once the initial enthusiasm wears off, any life-style
which does not have the support of the nonenthusiastic sociological
factors undergirding normative religion is hard to sustain. But those
who have been in and out may still retain a degree of interest or
even nostalgia, and the intermingling of these people with the
"world" helps to diffuse the religion's influence.

The other side of excursus religion's noncompetitiveness is a kind of diffuse influence which is very different in kind from that of normative denominations. Very few "standard" denominations—Methodist, Baptist, Roman Catholic—can be said to have had the widespread, noninstitutionalized yet highly identifiable influence on the art, literature, and intellectual life of non-members that Western Zen or even the Shakers have had. Very few "mainline" churches have the high percentage of occasional participation by non-members of Spiritualism, theosophical lectures, or yoga centers. This style of occasional, nonaffiliative participation is different from what would be practiced with regard to a "rival" denomination because of excursus's noncompetitive image. Innumerable non-Hindu Americans meditate in the Maharishi's manner or do yoga—but very few non–Roman Catholics say the rosary, and very few synagogues have a regular plurality of non-Jewish visitors. There is a good deal of dual or multiple membership, and even more of participation, in non-normative religious circles.

This diffuse influence is no less important when it is only extended through reading and involves no group participation at all. Many clergymen have known parishioners who, in terms of attendance, contributions, and donations of time to countless committees and activities were surely pillars of the church, to confess—often with a certain trepidation in the presence of the cloth—to a private love of Zen or Theosophical literature. Writings in the New Thought or positive thinking tradition, as well as certain evangelical authors, of course, have a comparable cross-sectarian appeal, but one does not easily imagine a staunch Lutheran nourishing a secret passion for Baptist books. Rather, reading interests represent an American religious map with contours ill-defined but doubtless widely differing from those of official denominationalism, and one in which the true strength of emergent religion would be better plotted than in church statistics.

It should be noted that these two facets of emergent and non-normative religion, the intensive and the diffuse, correspond well with the two forms Ernst Troeltsch gave to what he called mysticism, the immediate spiritual experience which in his sociological analysis of religion formed a "third type" of expression beside church and sect. Mysticism, he said, may be spoken of in a "narrow, technical, concentrated sense," a form which undercuts structures and forms new groups; and there is a "wider form" of mysticism that is diffuse and supports existing groups as well as deepening experience.[12] If groups in the emergent tradition represent reifications of Troeltschean mysticism, within its specific forms, such as yoga or Zen, can be found a "narrow" and a "wider" or diffuse expression.

A second important area of sociological interest is leadership. In excursus religion, the founding and, to a great extent, the continuing leadership is charismatic; even if, as in many Spiritualist churches, there is a great show of routinization in the elaborate constitutions and hierarchies, the real focus is the charisma of the mediumistic minister. The charismatic personality in emergent religion is one who has personally and paradigmatically undergone excursus. Like the shaman of old, and the magus who might be called a "shaman in civilization," he or she has made a passage through liminality, even perhaps initiatory psychopathology, and returned with remarkable spiritual credentials. So it was with Ann Lee, Madame Blavatsky, and many Spiritualists and Zen masters.

The crisis of the second generation—of continuing a movement after the passing of the charismatic founder and the original enthusiasts sparked by his or her fire—is especially acute in causes where there is little social reinforcement. It has been handled in various ways, but generally by means which enable the religion to continue as an excursus—that is, as a faith which draws people seeking an initiatory experience rather than taking up the family and community identity roles of religion—though inevitably, in the course of the transition, the excursus has become standardized and the leadership has become professional. Yet they may or may not differ significantly in their style from that of the first generation. Spiritualism has managed to retain something of its original character in each generation through the appearance of new mediums little different from those who have gone before. Zen also has a self-replenishing charismatic leadership in principle, though the training process is quite stylized. Theosophy has become quite definitely changed in the direction of routinization in its second and especially third generations of leadership, no longer claiming the sort of charisma and transcendent communication of its founders, but content simply to propagate its teachings.

It may also be noted that excursus religious groups have most of the general characteristics of withdrawal groups: a tendency to reach isolated people or a single status class (young people, older women, and so on), rather than the families and demographic cross-sections one would expect ethnic or community religions to reach; easy but definite entry procedures; provision for meaningful participation by nearly all members (or at least serious members) in responsible as well as receiving roles.

How is this sociology enacted in the praxis of the excursus religious group? The noncompetitive stance is typically maintained by advancing (particularly in the diffuse promotion) a single, simple practice which can produce fairly immediate and perceptible subjective change and can be practiced alone or in a small, ad hoc group quite independent of the kind of elaborate activities and structural ramifications of the parish church. Meditation, yoga, mediumship, chanting, and exciting concepts like those of Theosophy (as much as anything, this last is a spiritual way in which the transformative power comes from simply thinking over mind-expanding ideas) would be examples. These techniques are not for the sake of social identity even when done privately, like the Muslim prayer, but for their intrinsic effect on the doer.

Also, the excursus religion will have some practices which simply reify the excursus experience. That experience is one of separation, liminality, and reincorporation as a body in another context; its rituals, especially those of initiation, may mimic it. One thinks of those Neo-Pagan and Witchcraft groups which mount impressive "classic" initiations, even to blindfoldings and mild scourgings. More likely, the ceremonies are simply rites of identity, giving one status in the group and demarcating the group from outside society. They will define the set-apart order, as does Zen with its robes; or establish a group and place identity, as does pilgrimage to India or Japan; or create an assembly with a special state of consciousness, as does the long, rapid group chanting of Nichiren Shoshu of America. These practices, in contrast to those discussed in the preceding paragraph which are related to diffuse distribution, tend to form an intensive group or express the existence of one.

Finally, a few reflections on the theoretical expression of excursus religion. Almost by definition, it is a gnosis—a wisdom which has of itself, when truly known and acted upon, a saving power, which was always true but known only to an elect and now is again revealed to those with ears to hear. The gnosis concept correlates, of course, with the sociology of a small withdrawal group.

Beyond this, the teachings are diverse, yet certain themes are widespread. Generally we have an ultimate monism, but between it and this world of toil and shadows is spread what might be called an intermediate polytheism: an assemblage of masters, spirits, buddhas, gods, or archetypes who give texture and color to the One, and who can reach down to guide pilgrims along the way. This cosmology is, of course, characteristic of strong grid and group societies such as India, China, or medieval Europe; it offers a model both of cohesion into oneness and of hierarchy. It also offers an excellent paradigm of the excursus experience. It suggests an ultimate unity and many possible avenues of excursus toward it; its intermediate figures are generally lords once human who have advanced much further down the infinite way—but who can turn back with a word of hope and a helping hand.

The emphasis on creation is slight; the excursionist has instead in view an eternal, though perhaps evolving, world. Indeed, in our age of historical consciousness, he will probably see the internal transformation he has wrought through intellectual realization and the effect of the technique as the first fruits of a new age. From the Shakers onward, most excursus religion in America has had an eschatological thrust, linked to the current secular dream as well as to the tradition's ruminations about mystical evolution.

Yet another interesting form of expression, as much praxis as theoretical, has been a renewal of cosmic religion. From the "Holy Hills" and seasonal "cleansings" of the Shakers, to the sensitivity to nature of Zen and the explicit cosmicism of modern Neo-Paganism, the excursus journey has been not only toward the infinite but also toward a return to a sacred earth it feels the Judeo-Christian tradition has too much slighted. There is an uneven yet meaningful trend toward demarcating sacred space and time with seasonal rites, and even sacred centers. To be sure, American Christianity has managed to recover the Samhain, Yule, and Beltane of the Puritan's pagan forebears in the festive celebrations of Thanksgiving, Christmas, and Easter. But various excursus groups have gone on to schedule meditations or rites by the waxing and waning of the moon, not to mention the arcane dictates of astrology.

Moreover, whether in UFO cults or Buddhism, there seems to be a desire to recover the powerful religious meaning that holy places, places charged with power and worthy of pilgrimage, can have. American Christianity (unlike that of the Old World) has lost all sense of sacred places, but that has not deterred others. The UFO-related Aetherius Society has "charged" a number of sacred mountains in this land. As I was writing this chapter, I received a mailing from Feraferia, a colorful Neo-Pagan movement, indicating that it has established a "Ley Line" like those so much beloved of British esotericists.[13] But this one, extending for some 450 miles in California, is marked at regular intervals by Reichian orgone accumulators.

Symbols of Excursus

Peter Berger and Thomas Luckmann, in *The Social Construction of Reality*, have described the socioreligious process of projection, reification, and internalization. Feelings, anxieties, dualisms, and ecstasies within are projected and given body as the images, rites, structure, and common ideologies of a social order. These, on the wings of the language that names them, are then internalized as symbols through which one thinks and names oneself. Within and without, symbols are the religious coin of the realm.[14]

This model is viable so long as one realizes that the chain is unending, that religion no more "begins" in the subjectivity that is projected than it does in the outer reifications which are then internalized to create a modified subjectivity to be projected again. It should not be viewed as a reductionistic explanation, but rather as a description which simply acknowledges the ceaseless interaction of human inwardness, society, and cosmos to which religion gives voice. In this light, then, let us elicit some further symbols of excursus religion which accent its particular kind of human experience.

A very basic symbol is the group. In all social religion, of course, the sociological expression is highly symbolic. But in the case of excursus religion, beginning as it does with individual sense of alienation and call, the very existence of a group is in itself a powerfully important symbol. The immense significance of forming a group, however tiny or ephemeral, is evident all through the tradition, with its plethora of titles, charters, and post office boxes. Any entitled group, however small, is very different from an individual religious quest. Even the spiritual relation of only two people, master and disciple or two fellow seekers, is quite distinct from the subjectivity of a solitary soul, however expansive. The existence of any sort of group gives the experience a putative legitimation and a standing within the fabric of society as a whole which individual religion does not have in the same way; it may even be seen as the distinction between legitimate religion and madness.

In America, the group not only gives the religion a legal footing, but authenticates it as a part of our pluralism and a vindication of constitutional freedom in a public way. The group satisfies an implicit feeling that all real religion *ought* to have something in all three forms of religious expression, and it gives the religion a safety valve against spiritual inflation; it does not only exist in liminality, but must also be able to handle the things of this world regarding its corporate life. The leader must be able to control, like a shaman, his ventures to the other side, in such a way that he can also manage budgets, by-laws, and cantankerous individuals. All of this, our attitudes proclaim, indicate he is not a schizophrenic visionary, but one who has passed through the initiatory psychopathology to become a legitimate exerciser of religious freedom—and this social attitude is internalized by the religionists to make them want to reify and legitimate their vision in a group and in its accoutrements—buildings, offices, covenants, and stationery.

Within the religion, other symbols of excursus are evident. We have mentioned the recovery of cosmic religion, with all its rich symbols of sacred space and time, which sometimes occurs. We have also mentioned the rebirth of functional polytheism on the "intermediate" level. We could also cite a corresponding plurality of paradises or paradisal visions which emerge in the lore and art of excursus religion—a perception of "many mansions" on the other side, or of paradisal possibilities in terrestial nature. Almost imperceptibly, the last merges into social utopianism, the ideal of the "peaceable kingdom."

Especially in America, a significant symbol of excursus religion is feminine leadership and even feminine identity in the divine. In "mainline" American churches feminine clerical or professional leadership has never been more than nominal, and in the day when the Shakers, Spiritualists, Theosophists, and Christian Scientists were emerging with substantial feminine leadership, was virtually nonexistent. More important still, the characteristics of these movements clearly include signs of a quest for an authentic feminine spiritual identity—a quest reflected in the concepts of divinity itself, as in the bipolar masculine and feminine deity of the Shakers and the Christian Scientists; and in the typically "maieutic" rather than forensic concept of spiritual process. Even Zen has had, in America, a greater degree of feminine leadership than established churches.

A symbol of a somewhat different sort is wandering. Excursus religionists, especially the founders, leaders, and intensive practitioners, tend to be peripatetic. But "not all who wander are lost," and the seeming vagrancy has meaning. It is, as we have seen, first a symbol of liminal experience and status. Second, it may be in the nature of pilgrimage, like the journey of Blavatsky and Olcott to India, and so express not only liminality but also another symbol, an exotic place or remote holy land which encapsulates the otherness the excursus seeks. Third, as in the case of Johnny Appleseed and a Zen master in America like Soyen Shaku, it may disseminate the religion throughout the land by making the wandering a part of the message, inasmuch as the personality of the communicator is a part of it.

Still another symbol is the controlled use of trance or meditation. We have discussed ambiguities regarding trance in connection with grid and group. While the casual welcoming of trance in the original post-independence weak group and grid spiritual situation made possible its employment by early Spiritualists and their Mesmerist antecedents, in excursus religion trance is controlled in ways which legitimate its charismatic lineages. But in that context it is most important, for it then symbolizes the possibility of intrapsychic reflection of the strong grid and group cosmos and of subjective communication with it. In a word, it speaks of the possibility of unmediated and tangible ultimate transformation.

This brings us to the next topic, one which is linked to sociology by the social symbolic meaning of meditation: the psychology of excursus religion. To that we shall now turn.

3 Inner Worlds The Psychology of Excursus Religion

From Mount Shasta to Other Planets

The "I Am" Movement, famous in the thirties and early forties, and still active through several groups, was started by Guy Ballard and his wife. In 1930 Ballard, a mining engineer, was hiking on the slopes of Mount Shasta in northern California when he had an experience which, he said, changed his life "so completely that I could almost believe I were on another planet, but for my return to the usual routine in which I had been engaged for months."[1] Shasta, a gorgeous and isolated snow-crowned volcano in the midst of dark forests, a natural "holy site," has long had a special fascination for American esotericists; around its base are now centers of at least a dozen groups who believe special "lines of spiritual force" are operative in the mighty peak's vicinity.

It was a very warm, lazy day, and Ballard often stopped to rest. At lunchtime he found a clear, cool mountain spring. Stooping to fill his cup, the engineer felt an "electrical current" pass over his body. Then, turning around, he saw a remarkable man who gave him a vitalizing drink superior to spring water and discoursed on philosophical matters.

This experience may be compared with that of Paul Twitchell, founder of Eckankar, a now-substantial spiritual movement which centers on soul-travel, effecting inward journeys to higher worlds. Twitchell reports that he was initiated in the practice while in India on a journey of spiritual seeking. He writes:

One evening I lay down in a hotel room in Srinagar with the hope that the following morning would find me making contact with a *rishi,* who

lived almost inaccessible to those like myself, who were seeking some
experience with God.

Almost as quickly as my eyes were closed, I awoke in the *Atma Sarup,*
the soul body, to find myself walking along a sandy beach where the
wild surf lashed the shore and a wind whipped the pines along the edge
of the strand.

Something about the landscape was ethereal and my pulse was quick-
ened by the thought that this was an out-of-the-body projection via the
dream technique. The colors, the invigorating air, and the beauty of
the pale, white clouds against an azure sky were beyond words. It
seemed as if there was God in everything.[2]

In these auspicious surroundings, as one might have expected,
Twitchell did meet his spiritual guide, clothed in light.

One more of many such accounts is that of Orfeo Angelucci, a
UFO contactee whose case was given considerable attention by
Carl Jung.[3] Angelucci tells us that Friday, May 23, 1952, started out
as an ordinary day.[4] But after he went to his swing-shift job at an
aircraft plant, he began to feel ill and peculiar. He reports that an
odd prickling sensation ran through his arms and up his back; he
had a slight heart palpitation and his nerves were on edge. He says
that he always felt that way just before an electrical storm, but that
night was clear and the stars were bright.

Shortly after midnight Angelucci drove home, exhausted. The
nervous tension increased. His eyesight became blurred and the
noise of traffic around him was oddly muffled. Then, continuing
along a deserted stretch of road by a river, he saw a brilliant light
descend. Almost in a state of shock, Angelucci stopped, left his car,
and approached it. He was greeted by friendly voices from another
world, and began a period of conversing and travel between
paradisal spheres in outer space with these extraterrestial guides.
Though unlike Ballard and Twitchell, he has founded no group of
his own, Angellucci has written books and been a regular speaker at
religiously-oriented UFO meetings; to this extent his experience has
led to institutional acceptance and a certain fame. When I heard
him at the Giant Rock Space Convention, he commented that upon
meeting the marvelous visitors, he felt an exaltation "as though
momentarily I had transcended mortality and was somehow related
to these superior beings," and that he then "felt another world, or
something akin to a whole other universe." Clearly, Angelucci

experienced an initiatory shock which enabled a jump from one paradigm or "reality" to another.

These three twentieth-century American examples suggest a basic psychological feature of those who are deeply involved in excursus religion, especially as founders or transmitters: they sense the existence of two worlds, an ordinary world and an alternative one of wonder and meaning, and they enjoy the rare privilege of moving between the two as visitors and envoys.

All serious religion, of course, has something of this dual reality. Ordinarily, however, the reality of the alternative is strongly sustained by powerful symbolic and institutional reinforcement. I myself was at one time close to an intensely, poignantly romantic Anglo-Catholicism. I often dwelt, as in an alternative world, in a fairyland Middle Ages of pilgrimage and piety somewhere between the Seven General Councils and Lyonnesse. This alternative was supported by the whole panoply of gothic imagination. Ecclesiastical architecture, church ceremonials, vestments, incense, and music were such as to make walking into the churches of this persuasion a sensuous as well as a subjective entry into the portals of another world.

Institutionalized excursus religion, especially in its intensive centers, may have symbolic and social reinforcement comparable to this. But in the initial phases of a new wave of its transmission— that is, in experiences like those of Ballard, Twitchell, and Angelucci—and for most of those reached by its diffuse influence, the external institutional support will not be present. Instead, the major phenomenon will simply be people who sense they are "different," or discover it through experiences like these. They experience a subjective turbulence and acute self-consciousness which seems to make them more complex than others. To put it another way, they have not only a social identity like everyone else, but also a dissonant non-social identity in some way not placed by the ordinary structures of society, which needs to be reified.

This awareness of two identities dwells in rich interaction with excursus and the perception of other worlds. It is related to the Hegelian excursion and return of the spirit—for that is a journey which, like the excursus of excursus religion, is essentially intrapsychic. Journeys to India, like that of Twitchell and, before him,

Olcott and Blatvatsky, are only symbolic reifications of what is at
base a journey in the mind to another world also in the mind. It is a
journey from one's social identity—the self comprised of family,
status, work, and so forth—to one's non-social identity, to another
"self" which seems to have nothing to do with these things. Social
identity correlates with establishment religion; non-social with
emergent.

Of course, a journey to the non-social identity can ultimately end
in a new social identity. As in the case of Guy Ballard, the new
social identity can be one as leader of an institutionalized movement which reifies and legitimates the non-social identity through
giving meaning to the experiences that created it. It can be within
the ongoing "cultic milieu" described by Balch and Taylor. The
sense of two identities, or, rather, the overcoming of the problem of
two identities, is projected in two ways: outwardly, in the search for
reification in symbol and social group; and inwardly, where voices,
visions, and states of consciousness seem to validate the world of the
alternative identity. It is with this second projection that we shall
now be concerned, though we cannot forget that the two sides
unceasingly interact.

Transits from World to World

Let us examine more closely the meaning of two identities and their
expression in excursus religion. What seems to be involved is, first,
a sense of an inner reality, or an inner reality in rapport with some
cosmic reality, which does not wholly correspond to the structures
of the world. The latter are imperfectly internalized, in that something is leftover inside—and perhaps outside as well—that does not
mesh with the internalized structures. Since humans are dissatisfied
with a lack of equilibrium between inner and outer, this is a
situation which cannot be endured. The solution is to project
inward or outward the "leftover" surface to make out of it a
structure which can then be reified and internalized.

This does not mean, though, that the nonintegrated inner reality
has no content. It will, in fact, be a constellation of memories,
associative feelings, and concepts that somehow have a life of their
own; This particular grouping balks at merging into "establish-

ment" social and conceptual patterns that would link it to an "official" ultimate reality. But it may not be until these attitudes and ideas find an appropriate excursus which somehow does this for them that they are themselves able to emerge into consciousness by the aid of its power. (For the term "emergent religion" suggests something emergent as out of a sea, and this is suggestive as an intrapsychic metaphor.) Often, the associative pattern will be one reaching far back into early childhood.

These are people for whom the establishment church may convey one set of childhood memories: the awesomeness of liturgy, coloring pictures of angels and saints in Sunday school, other children or young people in various sorts of activity groups. That church was always something structured, social, and connected with acquired concepts or beliefs, however much internalized. But reading, say, Theosophical literature, for some reason brings to the surface memories perhaps even earlier and probably very different in setting. In them one may be alone, dreamy or reflective, and close to nature and its powers.

Several years ago I talked with an adept in ceremonial magic. He said that he viewed the evocational rite as the induction of a temporary, therapeutic schizophrenia, when real but intrapsychic entities could be called forth, given face and form, and commanded. He said also that the magical arts brought back the sense of wonder one had as a child.

Again, these unassimilated corners of the psyche which take religious expresssion may burst out as the sheer emotional ventilation of some Satanist rites, or create the kingdom of the gods in the fantastic rituals of Neo-Paganism. The point is they are manifestations of something long-standing in the individual's psyche not synchronized to the ordinary structures; something related to the ultimates with which religion deals and so calling for religious symbols; and something which makes a person feel sufficiently "different" that non-normative religion best bespeaks not only the psychic content but also the relation, or rather lack of relation, to society's norms that the realization entails.

Yet alternative reality is not always there. In this respect it is identical with Turner's liminality. Many enter it occasionally; some are at least symbolically in it as a lifelong vocation. But generally the experience of other worlds means that one must make transitions, and, indeed, it is necessary to do so. As we noted in the preceding chapter, the legitimation of a religious experience by society requires that ability, for the adept must prove his sanity by being able to move from his other world to the practical world of social relations and business affairs, and back again.

Alfred Schutz, as a phenomenological sociologist, has developed William James's notion of "sub-universes," and given the process of moving in and out of them definitions of use to us.[5] Schutz presents the "world of everyday life" or "working" world as a subuniverse or "finite province of meaning" among countless others, but insists that it is the paramount one, the mode of experiencing oneself and the universe which is the point of reference for all others. Whether or not this means it has an ontological priority is a question outside the phenomenology of experience. But Schutz tells us there are other worlds—"the world of dreams, of imageries and phantasms, the world of scientific contemplation, the play world of the child, and the world of the insane." Each of these has a cognitive style distinctive to itself, and so creates realms of experience with inner consistency, although these are not compatible with the cognitive style of "working" or "everyday life."

What of the transition from the ordinary to one of these other realities? Schutz says the transition is accompanied by a sort of "shock." It is, he says, like falling asleep to enter the world of dreams, and awakening to leave it; it is marked by the signs which betoken suspension of ordinary belief—like those evident when a story is being told, or a game is being played, or a ritual begins with procession or drum.

In the case of the three men with whom we opened this chapter, the transition is evident. Two of them reported a strange electrical feeling, a sudden uncanny perception, and a definite sense of encountering something of another order. The third apparently assimilated his transition to the "shock" of falling asleep and entering the dreamworld. The convulsions of some shamans entering and leaving trance, and the "jerks" of trance mediums as they enter the world of spirit, are comparable.

These cases were allegedly spontaneous and unexpected. They

may, however, fit the research-supported argument of Ralph W. Hood that mystical experiences in nature occur when something suddenly appears which points to the "limits" of everyday reality, especially when the occurence is stressful but was not stressfully anticipated.[6] But what of those like the shaman's or medium's, or the ritualist's and meditator's, which are highly intentional? Are they of the same order?

Not exactly, of course. But it must be remembered that religion strives to obliterate this distinction as much as possible. The contrived transition of the faith's epigone must convincingly be an entry into the same alternative world whither its founder went in his paradigmatic transition, or else the point is lost.

For this reason religions use techniques and images which amount to "condensed symbols" of its paradigmatic experience or person, and also extensive repetition of ritual or rhetoric. These, almost like post-hypnotic suggestion, can trigger a response in a believer similar to that of the original experience, or his own first faith, even though the sign may be so condensed as to seem superficially different. Examples are chanting, liturgical drama, lectures employing suggestive images or calling up emotively powerful concepts used over and over, or even comparable words on the printed page. The seance atmosphere and the "jerks" of the medium, and the sharp clapper in the Zen meditation hall which calls one to mindfulness are also examples.

The difference between the original experience and its induced recapitulation is not that the former is genuine and the latter derivative. To think of it in original-spontaneous versus imitative-contrived language grossly oversimplifies. Our three cases would appear to bear that out, for it is clear that in content these experiences were simply reversions to ancient beliefs in masters, soul travel, or UFOs and superhuman visitants from the sky. On the other hand, one does not doubt that many of the many who have, in "I Am" and Eckankar, sought to repeat Ballard's contact of ascended masters or Twitchell's out-of-the-body travel have had experiences which, to their own satisfaction, validated the goal and seemed to them as fresh and real as the paradigm. The fact that it was later in chronological time did not mean that it had all the connotations of "derivative." Subjective experience has only a

nodding acquaintance with clocks and calendars at best, and what is
real to it is neither more nor less real because of its relation to
another experience, or to the means by which it was triggered.
Whether one understands its induction to have been by a deliberately learned technique like those taught by "I Am" or Eckankar,
or by an unconscious trigger and projection of some sort, or, for
that matter, by supernatural intervention, may not, after all, say
much about the quality of the actual experience once it is released.

The nature of the triggering, then, may not determine the
essence of the experience as transition to another "world" where one
realizes a non-social identity. What it does determine, of course, is
the relation of that identity to one's social identity. One will be
drawn to triggering methods—or to unconscious "triggerings"—
which promise a realization of a non-social identity quite similar to
one's own, so much so one hopes for no dissonance between the
two. If one adapts a learned triggering, then one has a certain set of
social identity options available: as private practitioner, or as
member of a group which reinforces the transition in its own ways,
possibly tending to over-routinize it. If one has a "spontaneous"
experience, one may either keep it to oneself, or take up the
prestigious but lonely burden of the prophet.

Divine Madness

At several points we have alluded to comparisons between contact
with other worlds in the excursus religionist's subjectivity, and
"temporary schizophrenia," in the words of the magician. The
comparison with madness is highly suggestive, and certainly worth
exploring, in light of controversial contemporary views of insanity
which recognize in it therapeutic as well as destructive possibilities,
and recall the "divine madness" of Plato.

R. D. Laing is the best-known exponent of the new view of
madness.[7] His thesis is that what we call ordinary reality—the
"working" reality of Schutz—is in itself schizophrenic. Its structures create distortions of human personality which "work"
because they are reinforced by society, but only at great cost in
inhibition and pain to individuals. To become mad is the only way
many sensitive persons can deal with the greater madness around

them, and often the private madness produces a world which is not only better suited to them than the outer insanity, but also gives them a self-knowledge and inner strength that finally enables them to live better in an insane world.

According to Laing and his school, then, the real task of the psychotherapist is not to coerce the patient to accept his or society's or the psychiatric profession's opinion of what "reality" is, but accompany him or her on the trip through madness. Like Normon O. Brown's Dionysiac personality, his id and ego unite to create a personality dynamic enough to defy "reality," rather than developing a Freudian ego which accepts the reality-principle.

In reading Laing's work, one is impresssed by how often his patients seem to undergo religious and occult experiences. It is not only that, as Carl Jung recognized some time ago, the symbols in the minds of the mentally disturbed, like those in dreams, often show convergence with the archetypes of religious myth and rite. The passage of some of Laing's people through their psychoses, including contact with supernormal entities along the way, also parallel in structure traditional ritual and spontaneous initiations.

Laing describes one woman at his Kingsley Hall in London who regressed through childhood to infancy and even to the fetal state. She said she wanted to go all the way back to find herself, and live in a way that was not false. She reached a point where she was no more than a bundle of bones, had to be helped to take food and to defecate, and was often near physical death. Then she returned to adulthood gradually over a period of several weeks as a new person with a new personality.[8] The parallel to what is symbolized by religious rituals of death and rebirth, such as baptism, and to the more spontaneous initiatory ordeals of shamans and magi, is striking.

Even more striking in the present context is Laing's account of a former seaman who had a complete mental breakdown and had to be hospitalized for ten days. During this time he seemed helpless and dissociated. But although he could not communicate it to anyone, his experience during the breakdown was dramatic. At the depth of his outward decline, he felt he touched a source of power within himself, and had a sense of being on an immense journey through eons. Moreover, the patient felt that above reigned

not only God, but also intermediate beings like gods "far above us
capable of dealing with the situation that I was incapable of dealing
with, that were in charge and were running things, and at the end
of it, everybody had to take on the job at the top."[9]

This decription and the pilgrimage through the eons in countless
reincarnations, culminating in the right and duty of being a lord of
cosmic destiny, seems an apparently spontaneous re-creation in
mental crisis of the Theosophical world view. In it the Masters, like
the Bodhisattvas and Rishis and Sufi "Pivot Saints" of classic
Eastern lore, are human beings developed tremendously beyond
the norm and are the benign administrators of the invisible government of the world.

If one were to examine the initiatory experiences of many in
excursus religion, especially those in it intensively, one would probably find nonclinical and better controlled parallels to these; even
experiences of those reached by excursus religion's diffuse influence
perhaps represent "miniaturizations" of these breaks and rebirths
through manipulation of subjective "condensed symbols." Again,
whether the process is spontaneous-seeming, as in the case of the
founders of "I Am" and Eckankar, or learned and induced, as for
the ceremonial magician, is not of critical importance from the
psychological perspective. In both cases it may be a working
through "madness" and learning from it. It is developing and
stabilizing and giving substance to one's non-social identity as a foil
against the opposing "madness" of the society which informs one's
social identity. The excursus religionist is aware in his own way of
the drab, one-dimensional quality, even the schizophrenia, of mass
society and its prevailing world views.

While this is not the place to discuss the theoretical validity of
Laing's hypotheses, which have certainly not gone unchallenged, I
think it is fair to say that they offer an unusual and illuminating
insight into the inner experience of excursus religion and the subjective face of its tension with society. In Laingian terms, perhaps the
ideal would be, as we have suggested, to find the point of precise
equilibrium, a Buddhistic middle way, between the outer madness
of society and the inner madness of unbridled subjective excursus,
so that one could draw the strength and perspective of each as a
corrective to the other, without being trapped in the black hole of

each alone. This is the way of the magus who, like Castaneda's Don Juan, has a shamanistic "lightness" which enables him to move between worlds, manage practical as well as transcendent affairs, and keep his balance on the thin edge of interfacing realities.

The Modern Magus

A person who maintains this equilibrium between sub-universes possesses a peculiar fascination. He shimmers with a certain glamor, as though his life was itself a mystic spell. Like all magic, it may be partly illusion, but one is drawn back to the thaumaturge time and again because one is never quite sure what is sleight-of-hand and what is really a glimpse into some alternative universe—or whether even the sleight-of-hand may not have some significance beyond trickery. Like the shaman of old, the adept is mainly concerned with creating a universe of meaning in which the spiritual reality that he believes in is perceived as the absolute and fundamental truth. This means that it must be reified as evident truth on all levels of perception so that no crack is left for cognitive dissonance. If that end requires certain technical adjustments to maintain consonance in the world of such gross senses as outward sight and hearing, those adjustments are not very different from the belief-fomenting glamor of any rhetoric or symbol-manipulation.

As in the case of the shaman, neither words nor ecstatic scenario nor trickery nor wake of myth and wonder are in themselves the shamanistic mastery of equilibrium. The shaman-in-civilization, whom I have previously referred to as the "magus," and who is the mainstay of the emergent and excursus religious traditions, actually comes into being in and through relationships.[10] The transformative catalyst he becomes for the circle around him is more important than what he says or does, in itself. The most significant feature of the charismatic figure, the magus, is that he becomes a symbol in the minds of others—a symbol that is powerful enough to effect a reordering of the disciple's mindset, to raise or lower the threshold of the unconscious, or to "cleanse the doors of perception" so that modalities or patterns of reality are seen which were not before. The words of the magus are important, but important because of their associative power rather than what a strict and

detached intellectual analysis might prove about them; the wonders
he is alleged to have accomplished are significant, yet the question
of whether they would be verifiable under laboratory conditions is
not really to the point—the important thing is that in the context
of the relationship they become symbols and bearers of the transcendence incarnate in the magus. Remarkable spiritual figures from
Jesus to Madame Blavatsky have worked extraordinary phenomena
as signs in the context of interaction with followers, but have not
commanded stones to become bread to meet their own private
needs outside that context, despite much provocation.

This sort of relationship, whether with a wonder-worker or a Zen
master who simply shows uncanny insight into one's psyche, marks
the difference between the magus of the excursus path and the
philosopher or clergyman. It is not so much different ideas that set
them apart as it is different relationship styles marked by different
symbols of the meaning of the relationship. There is a distinction
between the philosophies of Alfred North Whitehead and the
Russian mystagogue Georges Gurdjieff, even though both expounded a process philosophy which drew from the wells of
platonism and both were interested in mathematical symbolism.
There is probably some difference in their respective competence
with the tools of the philosopher's trade. But a major difference
between the two is that while, to the best of my knowledge, there
are no groups devoted to Whitehead's thought outside academic
circles, Gurdjieff has scores of groups devoted to discussing his
philosophy and practicing the "work" that accompanies it. Both
philosophers have had influence, but it has differed in kind, owing
to the very different nature of the relationship between the mentor
and the followers and that relationship's symbolic meaning for the
latter.

It would be instructive to compare those men of ideas whose
influence has taken the form of shaping intensive groups and a
sense of master-disciple relationships—like the Buddha, Gurdjieff,
and even Teilhard de Chardin—and those, like Aristotle and Whitehead, in which it has not. For the former, the master becomes
internalized as a transcendent symbol around which aspects of the
psyche governing several levels of activity—social, motor, even
memory and ego-formative—become arranged. For the latter, the

philosopher is a person with important ideas. In that cleavage lies the distinction between philosophy and religion.

The difference surfaces basically in two factors: a different personality on the part of the mystagogue and a different technique. We have cited the glamor and mystery, the sense of being on the border of realities, borne by the magus. We have also mentioned his capacity to be internalized as a subjective symbol in the minds of his followers. What this really means is that his personality, his image, becomes a condensed symbol of more than himself— whether of the experienced history of him in relation to the disciples, that is, of the relation itself; or of a particular kind of transcendence; even, like Teilhard, of a spiritual generation.

The second difference is in technique. While the academic philosopher will use and teach only intellectual techniques, the religionist will work in all three of the forms of religious expression. He will use non-intellectual techniques of communication and reinforcement, and will probably teach sensual and motor means of self-incorporation into the transcendence he mediates.

What makes a person a mystagogue? Whether a Ballard, Twitchell, or Angelucci, a Gurdjieff or Blavatsky, he is a person marked by experiences of liminality and even initiatory madness, probably symbolized by wandering and visions or voices; he is a person whose non-social self has a life of its own and the power to form its own society.

Consider Helena Blavatsky, the dominant figure in nineteenth-century Theosophy. Though she was brought up in aristocratic circles in Orthodox Russia, and though she occasionally had wistful yearnings toward conventional faith and life, the major features of her inner life were occult initiations, communication with transcendent masters, and the paranormal powers they worked through her—all of which created in her a non-social self that could only be socialized through new sets of relationships centering on its own phenomena.

This personality was intertwined with a long-standing sense of alienation from society and tension from it. This quality as it expresses itself in the life of the magus of excursus religion has rarely been better or more forcefully expressed than in a letter Blavatsky wrote in 1884 to the Russian writer Vselovod S. Solovyoff, at a time when charges of fraud had been published against her under the auspices of the British Society for Psychical Research and many had turned away from her. Solovyoff, brother of the mystical philosopher Vladmir S. Solovyoff, had been in Blavatsky's confidence for a period in 1884. Despite their friendship, he published this letter, albeit with her permission, together with other correspondence and memoirs in a book, *A Modern Priestess of Isis*, intended as an exposé of the mysterious madame. Combined as it is with Solovyoff's rather priggish moralizing about his enigmatic countrywoman, this publishing venture has its distasteful aspect. Nevertheless, much of the material, as Solovyoff recognized, is of great psychological interest.

In the letter, Madame Blavatsky first asks the reader to picture in the mind this scene. "There is living in the forest a wild boar—an ugly creature, but doing no harm to any one so long as they leave him in peace in the forest, with his wild beast friends who love him." But this comrade of the wild things is suddenly turned upon by a pack of fierce hounds, and has no choice but to turn and "show himself wholly as he is, from top to bottom," as he attacks back at the horde until he falls.

She goes on to say that she will write a full confession of her life, and gives a few hints of what that document will contain, combining allusions to great turpitude with claims about the immense good her Theosophy has done. Then she says "I will even take to lies, to the greatest of lies, which for that reason is the most likely of all to be believed. I will say and publish it in the *Times* and in all the papers, that the 'master' and 'Mahatma K. H.' are only the product of my own imagination: that I *invented* them, that the phenomena were all more or less *spiritualistic* apparitions ... I will say that in certain instances I *fooled* people; I will expose dozens of *fools* ..."[11]

Here we see an attempt at self-understanding by a complex personality whose non-social self is powerful yet needs expression through the medium of some sort of relationship. Solovyoff later says, "She imagined that everything in the world was founded on personal relations, and that to this there was no exception." She sees herself as set against the world, friend only of the strange and wild, with powers capable of great depravity and great good. She has an immoderate capacity for self-dramatization, and the temptation to lie and deceive is always there and doubtless sometimes indulged, yet always in the context of something else which is not a lie but is almost impossible to communicate about, so much is it a part of the non-social self. Yet communicate it she must, for the something else paradoxically must grow in relationships, even if it has roots in experiences closer to the private heavens and hells of those bruised and blessed by initiatory madness.

In personalities like those of Blavatksy, Gurdjieff, and many another luminary of counterspirituality, one observes qualities not only of the paradigmatic shaman and magus, but also of the trickster and "ritual clown." The trickster is that figure in many mythologies who cleverly outwits both gods and men and manages to establish a precarious immortality for himself on the tenuous boundary between heaven and human society. From that outsider's vantage point he laughs at the pomposity and gullibility of both realms.

In many human communities something of the same role is taken by the trickster's emulators, the ritual clowns who may follow an uplifting performance by priest or shaman with a comic burlesque of it, or even interrupt sacred solemnities with rough humor and obscenities. Those holidays which, like Purim or Carnival or the Hindu Holi, treat religion in a light vein have much the same role, and their traditions, like the clowns, have been thought ultimately important to cosmic (and human) equilibrium.

The strange ways, defiance of conventional morality, and mockery of normative faith for which many colorful figures outside normative spirituality are notorious can be put in trickster perspective, among others. Those with this quality are not likely to be long idolized by many. At the same time, the sport they make of the solemn assemblies of established religion—sometimes with the raucous derision of a Blavatsky, sometimes without scornful words but only by showing an alternative way—is often salutary. Even the dangerous disregard of ordinary virtue may, especially when that virtue is overlaid with sanctimoniousness, have its point. Heinrich Zimmer, in *Myths and Symbols in Indian Art and Civilization*, writes of "that touch of 'amorality' which must form at least part of one's intellectual and intuitive pattern, if one is not to fall prey to predetermined bias and be cut off from certain vital, highly ironical, and disturbing insights."[12]

Meditation and Expansive Consciousness

In the psychology of excursus religion, special attention must be given to meditation, since in the American scene it has played such an important role. Varying definitions have been given for meditation, but generally the crucial point is that in meditation the consciousness is directed away from outward things and reflected back upon itself—upon particular sacred images or thoughts which are conjured up in the mind, or upon the formless essence of consciousness, or even upon a simple observing of the ordinary processes of thought. This act properly becomes "one-pointed," to use the Eastern term, in that it gives rapt attention in the present to its focus, excluding all else. The process may be aided by posture, or even dance, and by sensory stabilization through attention to a single sight or sound. The meditation act should induce a tranquil or ecstatic state of consciousness. It may deepen into the trance of mediums and others, or broaden to include work or play done with a rapt but calm state of attention, especially when these are interpreted as religious states.

Meditation is not, of course, unknown to the Judeo-Christian religious tradition, and has a part in the traditional spirituality of the Roman Catholic and Eastern Orthodox churches particularly. Undoubtedly much Judeo-Christian prayer is psychologically not very different from meditation. But it must be conceded that meditation is attention to consciousness itself, whereas prayer is psychologically and symbolically structured as an "I-thou" relation to a personal God conceived of as essentially outside the psyche. This is a problematic but not insuperable matter, as Christian mystical theology and kabbalistic Jewish thought concerning meditation shows. However, it has meant that in religion in which meditation is central—in Judaism and Christianity it has always been at best a sort of "option" for a minority of mystical bent, and has not seldom been regarded dubiously—the tendency is inevitably toward an immanentialist and monistic ontology oblique to much Western religious experience, especially as represented in the "establishment" churches.

This has meant that for Western non-normative religion, meditation has often been very important, a prime tacit symbol of that religion's oppositional character. The reasons are threefold.

First, meditation offers an excursus for those to whom the whole meditation experience is alien. Whatever its ontological validity, in a culture structured around interpersonal meanings on both the terrestrial and cosmic planes, meditation focusing on one's own inwardness presents a new and wonderful world. That is all the more the case when intersubjective meanings appear to relate only to the expression of one's social self, and the non-social self is left with no appropriate venue—unless meditation inflates it until it momentarily attains the dignity of being virtually the whole.

Second, meditation, whether in Eckankar, TM, or Spiritualism, serves as an important symbol of an alternative spirituality. In itself, the practice of meditation symbolizes that one is engaged not in a religion that mainly cements family or community bonds, or places one in a cosmic interpersonal relationship, but in a religion that involves deep internal exploration and the modification of states of consciousness to actualize that true self which, presumably, one will find at the end of the quest. Because the presuppositions and language of meditation are different, its practice symbolizes— above all to oneself—that one's adventure is different. Sociologically, a serious interest in meditation will inevitably align one, in America, with different kinds of people than will a major interest in "establishment" religion.

Third, meditation or something like it is essential to excursus religion because it can give that sense of immediacy and cosmic participation necessary to counter the sociological pressure to conform to the establishment religion of one's culture. A bare ideology, or even rite, is not sufficient to stand against those forces; they must be met with an equal subjective impetus that is to a great extent self-validating.

All these reasons for meditation's importance in American excursus religion can be summed up in the concept of meditation as expansive consciousness—expansive as a movement toward the

Other Side, and as a foil against pressures to conform to established religion.

Polymorphous Sensuality

Still another interesting set of psychological correlates can be found for excursus religion—a set that concerns the senses employed. Ernest G. Schachtel, a psychoanalyst, has distinguished the "proximity senses"—touch, taste, smell—from the "distance senses" of hearing and sight, and explained that in early childhood we make a partial transition from concentration on the former to concentration on the latter.[13] This creates a new and more extended environment, but one in which the person is less immediately involved as a psycho-physical organism.

If a religious map of America, or of the world, were drawn along the lines of whether distance or proximity senses were dominant, it would be different from the maps drawn to demarcate formal beliefs, and would be quite instructive. Magical rites and tantrism, for example, often include sexual rites and generally involve, as does sex, evocative use of the proximity senses. Catholic sacramental worship employs a rather genteel token acknowledgment of all the senses in its use of incense, kissing of holy objects, and bread, as well as icon and song and sermon. But classical Protestant worship suggests a vehement denial that meaningful religious communication can come through the proximity senses; it reflects "maturation" in its view that hearing and seeing (of the word, and of the unmediated reality of the creation) are alone reliable or sanctified.

Excursus religion, ranging as it does from magic and Neo-Paganism to highly ethereal "metaphysics," represents the whole sensory gamut. But it is worth noting that a tendency toward recovering the sacred possibilities present in the whole sensory spectrum often emerges. Even in a movement like Pentecostalism, as in Spiritualism, Theosophy, and Zen, a barely veiled sensuality lurks just beneath the spiritual surface, expressing itself in "phenomena," in unusual styles of marriage and community, in an ecstatic relation to nature.

Kenneth Grant, in his valuable and sympathetic study of modern ceremonial magic, and particularly in his work on Aleister Crowley, the notorious mage of the twenties and thirties, emphasizes the physical and physiological basis of magical phenomena and the extent to which its rites and symbols are shot through with tantralike sexual images. The power of magic, he indicates, really resides in the profound union of the person with his or her physical energies that it can effect; magic is a union of metaphysical concepts with psychodynamics, sexology, and endocrinology, all aligned to will. It is far from being only a "spiritual" matter. Indeed, Grant tells us, contrary to what some seem to believe, in initiatory mystery traditions like magic, it is the spiritual or philosophical explanations that are exoteric, concealing what are actually physiological experiences of great power, and not the other way around.[14] Magic and ritual seem to evoke a primal stage of human development when psyche and physiology were much more intimately integrated than after the distance senses, and the ego, began to create worlds of consciousness separate from the "world" of the physical body, its wordless energies, needs, and knowledges.

Not all excursus religions, of course, are as frank and full-blooded a return to primary sensuality as sexual magic. Some, rejecting even the tepid sacramentalism of conventional Christianity, appear only overspiritualizations of religion reinforcing body-spirit dualism. They are in the lineage of the ancient orphic and platonic allegorizing of physical aspects of initiatory and shamanistic ecstasy.

Yet it is interesting to note ways in which excursus religion, both in what it recovers and in what it too obviously represses, is sometimes an excursus toward an unconventional relationship with the senses and the sexuality so potently linked to them. The reader may wish to reflect on the proximity sense meaning of the virulent Shaker dance and spiritualism in the context of Shaker celibacy, the transparent sexual mysticism of Thomas Lake Harris, the recovery of tangible evidence in the "phenomena" of Spiritualism and of Madame Blavatsky, the association of the highly ceremonial Liberal Catholic Church with Theosophy, and the decorous exaltation of all five senses by conventional Zen, together with the paradoxical libertinism of some of its American "beat" devotees.

Let us end this chapter, though, with the observation that the real excursus of excursus religion is inward. The sociology, praxis, and doctrine, even the relation to the body and the senses, all finally serve only to symbolize excursus and to create a psychic space in which it can take place. In conventional religion these features often are the religion, in the sense that a major function of it is to provide social placing. This is also the case in excursus religion, in that the excursus may represent a liminal social position; but for this reason it has no power unless it provides a compensatory inner journey. The bulwarks of a different social group, actions, and beliefs free one to make this journey, which can be understood in terms of the platonic "divine madness."

2 Histories

4

Shakers and Spiritualists

An Ancient Sybil

According to the old sagas, at the Norse settlement of Herjolfsness in Greenland, an interesting event happened about the year 1000, shortly before Leif Eriksson's voyage to Vinland or America. A prophetess named Thorbjorg attended the winter feast of Thorkel, a farmer. She wore a blue mantel adorned with stones down to the hem. On her head was a black lambskin hood lined with white cat's fur, and she wore catskin gloves. Her staff was capped with a brass knob studded with stones, and from her belt of touchwood hung a large pouch full of the charms required for her craft. On her feet she wore hairy calfskin shoes with thick laces that had tin buttons on the ends. The evening of her arrival she ate a meal consisting largely of a gruel of goat's milk and a main dish made of the hearts of various animals; this she ate with a brass spoon, and a knife with a walrus-tusk handle.

Late the next day the sybil prepared to do her witchcraft. She needed the assistance of women familiar with the spells, known as warlock-songs, that would summon up spirits. None of the women present did, save a maiden of good family called Gudrid. But those were the days when Christianity was spreading among the folk of the North, and Gudrid, though she acknowledged that she had learned the warlock-songs from her foster mother Halldis in Iceland, declined at first to sing them, saying, "This is the sort of knowledge and ceremony that I want nothing to do with, for I am a Christian."

Other guests argued convincingly that singing the songs could not really hurt her, and might be of help to others. Finally, under pressure from Thorkel, the host, Gudrid acquiesced. Thorbjorg seated herself on a ritual platform, the other women forming a circle around that awesome feminine figure, and Gudrid chanted the mystic stanzas. It was said that none before had heard lovelier singing.

The prophetess thanked her, saying, "Many spirits are now present which were charmed to hear the singing, and which previously had tried to shun us and would grant us no obedience. And now many things stand revealed to me which before were hidden both from me and from others."

Thorbjorg, presumably in a state of mediumistic trance, then foretold the future. Looking into the days and years ahead, she perceived the imminent end of the famine and epidemic that had lately afflicted the pioneer community and saw a bright destiny for Gudrid. Then she gave individual readings for all present, said mostly to be accurate, and departed. A messenger was sent to summon back Thorbjorn, Gudrid's father, for he had refused to be present while such paganism was going on.[1]

As for Gudrid, she later married a certain Karlsefni and accompanied him to Vinland. There, the Graenlendinga Saga tells us, she dwelt in the tiny Norse settlement for a year and gave birth to a son, Snorri. She, and the other settlers, had difficult encounters with the Skraelings, as the natives were called. Though she remained resolutely Christian, once in Vinland she had a puzzling apparition of a short, pale woman with unforgettably large, luminous eyes who entered the house and, after asking Gudrid's name, introduced herself as Gudrid also. Was it a *döppelganger* or a projection of some alternative personality? Gudrid never learned, for just then she was interrupted by a loud noise from outside as Karlsefni's men killed a Skraeling who was trying to steal some weapons. The vision vanished and was not seen again. The party returned to Iceland.

Later, after the death of her husband and her son's marriage, the redoubtable Gudrid made a pilgrimage to Rome, and ended her days as an anchoress in Iceland. Two of her great-grandsons were bishops.[2]

Three points from this narrative of Norse spiritualism are striking in connection with our endeavor to understand the alternative altars of America. First, we may note the concentration of feminine spiritual force which empowered the sybil's seance. The medium was a woman; she was surrounded with a supporting ring of females; and only the song of a woman could soften the will of her spirits. Men might be (as some still argue today) the only acceptable ministrants at the altars of Christ, the new power; but in Thorbjorg's world the menfolk, however strong in battle, were only humble suppliants before the powers controlled by the other sex.

Second, we note the dimensions of the conflict between the religion of the spirits and that of Christ. The Norsemen were relatively tolerant for their day, but, even so, those like Thorbjorn who had forsaken the hammer of Thor for the cross were not at ease with such doings—though one senses in Gudrid, a woman and a Christian, an unconscious ambivalence, reflected in her ability to sing the shamaness's songs with unexpected force once her scruples were overcome. The conflict certainly did not die easily; memories of Thorbjorg's breed were undoubtedly brought much later to Massachusetts by the Norsemen's Anglo-Saxon cousins, and had an influence on certain events at Salem. And, as we shall see, this heritage—influenced also by the comparable shamanism of the Skraelings or Amerindians, and by many other lineages—was in a sense reborn in more liberal times in such American phenomena as Shakerism and Spiritualism, not to mention the tiny Witchcraft and Neo-Pagan movements of today.

Third, we note that Thorbjorg's message was one of a spiritual world immediately accessible, comprised of finite but pluralistic powers, and promising a future brighter than the present. We have already observed that these views of the spiritual world are characteristics of excursus religion generally, at least where the familiar religion is historical and monotheistic Christianity. They are particularly characteristic of Spiritualism.

Ecstatic Religion

Let us reflect a little more on the theme of sexual antagonism in religion. We should not overemphasize its importance in understanding excursus religion in America, for there are several other symbols of reversal of the ordinary that are of equal importance. But it should not be underemphasized either, particularly as a psychological dynamic. Consider how many new movements originated in America were founded by women—Shakerism, Spiritualism, Seventh-Day Adventism, Christian Science, Theosophy, Divine Science. Or consider those that, while founded by men, established unconventional relations between the sexes—the Latter-Day Saints (in its early polygamy), the Oneida Community. Or those, like the New Thought churches and Pentecostalism, that have had an unusually high proportion of women preachers and members. Virtually all the movements just named have a rich history of new revelation suggestive of spiritual immediacy triumphing over history, a spiritual cosmos more monistic or pluralistic (or both) than that of the Lord of Sinai, and a view of a new spiritual start in the New World and of a brighter future that often reaches apocalyptic proportions—even as did the oracles of Thorbjorg.

Whether, as Jungian analysts would argue, characteristics like these—drawn from the unity of the womb, the pluralism of the family under the maternal arms, and the apocalyptic process of giving birth—represent an inalienable feminine pattern of spirituality too long repressed is a matter beyond the scope of this book. Others would argue that it represents only the ecstatic and apocalyptic religion typical of oppressed groups who have little to hope from the reason, law, and hierarchical authority that cater to those dominant. Since the latter are invariably men, as well as of the proper race and class, we have no empirical grounds for saying what the religion of women would be like in other circumstances.

There is little doubt, though, that we are dealing with a recognizable phenomenon and set of associations. The predominance of women in ecstatic, possession, mystical, and healing cults is a worldwide fact. It is as evident in Haitian voodoo, the ancient Greek Dionysiacs, and the Japanese new religions, as in the somewhat more decorous Shakers, Spiritualists, Theosophists, and Pentecostalists of America.

I. M. Lewis, in *Ecstatic Religion*, gives a vivid account of the *zar* cults of Islamic East Africa. Women in this ostensibly highly masculine society will from time to time be possessed by vigorously assertive spirits which, through the mouths of the entranced wife or kinswoman, make demands on men. Although ordinarily the women obey rather than give orders, these importunities for gifts or favors are generally met, for the power of the spirits to bring misfortune to those who defy their wishes is well known.

Lewis argues that such cults are "thinly disguised protest movements directed against the dominant sex."[3] Excursus religion has certainly had such overtones for many. Madame Blavatsky of Theosophy once put it forcefully enough: "Woman finds her happiness in the acquisition of supernatural powers. Love is but a vile dream, a nightmare."[4]

Lewis also makes the significant point that the spirits involved in this type of feminine possession cult are not so much concerned with upholding the moral order of the established society—which, in any case, is probably a rationalized ethic supporting male hegemony—as they are with simply giving joy, ecstasy, excitement, healing, and an inchoate sense of countervailing power. They are, in other words, spirits embodying the flavor of an opposing, feminine liminal world. While the invisible communicators of American Spiritualism and related movements have, indeed, delivered reams of moral discourse, often replete with fulsome Victorian platitudes, on notable occasions their values have also seemed highly oblique, and the general sense one gets of the movement is that much of its real appeal lay less in what its otherworldly guides and teachers said than in the atmosphere of wonder and power that commerce with them exuded—though, of course, much the same can be said of any experience of the numinous.

Two Women: I

The shaman, as we have seen, is one who has passed through an initiatory madness, death, and rebirth, emerging in control of spirit helpers, able to transcend the boundaries between worlds, so that he can travel to or communicate with gods and departed souls and give boons of healing and divination to humankind. The shamanic paradigm leaps to mind as one reads about many important figures in the excursus religious tradition, but none recall it more effectively than two women who began their work on these shores when the nation was young.

It was in 1776 that the eighteen-year-old Jemima Wilkinson of
Cumberland, Rhode Island, appeared to die from the plague. Her
body grew cold and stiff. But then it became warm again, rose up,
and began to speak. And the voice that spoke through it confirmed
that, indeed, Jemima Wilkinson had "left the world of time," but
that her body was now to serve as the vehicle of the Spirit of Life
from God, and should be known as The Publick Universal Friend.

For forty-three years thereafter The Friend worked from within
that body. During the first fourteen of them she traveled about the
northeastern states calling upon the citizens to lead Christian lives
and winning converts. Her doctrine was generally orthodox enough,
save for a lack of respect for lawful marriage, for she often per-
suaded followers to leave spouses who were not equally dedicated to
The Friend, and came more and more to counsel complete chastity.
Hers was a dramatic presence well able to lure the hearts of impres-
sionable followers from earthly bonds. Strikingly tall, with ample
dark hair, passionate eyes, and lovely coloring, she wore a low white
beaverskin hat and a full white robe. She was accompanied by two
associates: Sarah Richardson, who was alleged to be "the prophet
Daniel operating in these latter days in the female line," and James
Parker, who, dressed in prophet's robes, gave voice to the spirit of
Elijah. At The Friend's open meetings, these persons would de-
claim, fall to the ground in rapture, or describe visions of heaven as
the Spirit gave them utterance, and The Universal Friend would
stand between them to plead the love of God with graceful gestures
and winning voice.

It can easily be believed that, though she had her share of
enemies and was even once tried (and acquitted) for blasphemy,
The Friend also won wealthy and prominent admirers and converts
and did not lack for this world's goods. Indeed, toward the end of
her traveling ministry, she had built for herself an open coach,
shaped like an upturned half-moon, with seats of gold tapestry,
and both on the front panels and over her head were engraved the
letters U.F. Many regarded The Spirit of Life from God as none
other than the returned Christ, an opinion she neither affirmed nor
denied.

In the early 1790s The Friend ceased traveling and settled with
260 followers pledged to obedience and celibacy in the Finger Lake
district of New York State. Here a community was built, centering

about a large, beautiful house for The Friend overlooking Lake Keuka. Here the mystic queen lived in state, waited on by seven maids of youth and beauty, and gave divine counsel to suppliants from near and far. She and her people reported frequent visions, wonders, and exchanges with the Other World out of time.

As years passed, though, dissensions and apostasy, especially in the matters of communal property and celibacy, racked the community. It was also weakened by the loss of the many who "left time," as the prophetess called dying, and were not replaced. The decades also left their mark on The Friend, whose fleshly vehicle came to know age and illness, much to her distaste. She once commissioned a portrait, then refused to allow it to be shown when the artist captured too honestly the ravages of the years on what was once a divine beauty.

Some stayed faithful until the end of her earthly course in 1819. Then certain adherents who had expected her to be immortal were distraught, and others were disappointed when she did not return after three days, as they had anticipated. But still others of the Jemimakins, as her devotees were called, continued by occult means to consult the spirit of The Publick Universal Friend for advice until at least the end of the century, and she is still a local legend, if not cult, around Yates County, New York.[5]

Two Women: II

In 1774, just two years before the transformation of Jemima Wilkinson, a tiny band under the leadership of another changed and chaste woman of prophetic gifts arrived in the New World. She was called Mother Ann Lee, and she was foundress of the United Society of Believers in Christ's Second Appearing, commonly called Shakers.

Ann Lee had been born in Toad Lane, Manchester, in 1736, amid the squalor of an eighteenth-century British industrial town. Her father, a blacksmith, was not prosperous; the child grew up without education and worked in a cotton factory from an early age. (Most of her first followers were of similar background; the idyllic rural communal life which became the Shaker ideal was not so much a product of the frontier, as a reaction to the notorious evils of the first industrial cities.)

Even as a child, Ann found the matter of sexual relationships extremely distasteful. We are told she often admonished her mother against the "impure" act, so that her father was driven to take up the whip. Nonetheless, she married a man named Abraham Stanley and had four children by him, all of whom died in infancy—she read those sad losses as a sign she was not called to cohabitation. After her children's deaths, she went through nine years of deep mental distress. The condition was, judging from the accounts, something more than simple depression. She would weep and moan through long sleepless nights, and wasted away to a virtual skeleton, weak as an infant. This stage can be compared to the archetypal shaman's initiatory pathology; the period was also "filled with visions and revelations of God."

Her process out of this divinely disturbed state was greatly aided by her becoming affiliated with the "Shaking Quakers," a small group of ecstatics on the fringes of Quakerism influenced by French Camisard refugees in England. Finding a sympathetic group in which one's own mental disturbances have sacred meaning can often transform those disturbances from weakness to sources of extraordinary strength. It can release new powers of leadership and creativity, while granting social legitimacy to what had been a private vision in conflict with the world's construction of reality. Thus in 1770, after uniting with the Shaking Quakers and, indeed, while in prison for her testimony on their behalf, she received after deep distress a "full revelation of the root and foundation of human depravity, and of the very transgression of the first man and woman in the garden of Eden."[6] (One is reminded of Sun Myung Moon, the visionary founder of the Unification Church, who perceived that the secret basic sin of Eden was that Satan had sexual relations with Eve.)

After her revelation, Mother Ann grew in strength and in the power of her testimony; before long she was effectual leader of the Manchester Shaking Quakers. Though she suffered much persecution from the officials, her course was set. Hers was to be a religion that combined that group's singing, dancing, "shaking," and ongoing ecstatic revelations, with sexual abstinence as the way of the kingdom of heaven. Her followers believed she was none other than the second appearance of Christ.

In 1774, following special revelations and promises from God,

Ann left for America with her husband, brother, and several other "Shakers." They settled at first in New York City, and quietly found work. Ann was employed as a laundress, but after a time had to stop work to care for her husband, who had become very ill. She was reduced to the depths of poverty, at one point having nothing but a cold room and, for nourishment, a cruet of vinegar. After his recovery her husband demanded cohabitation with his wife, and when she vehemently refused left her and the movement for good.

In 1776 the little flock settled at Niskayuna (now Watervliet) near Albany, New York. The territory was then frontier country, and there it was that the Shaker communal life had its beginnings. Their early history is one of hardships. Hunger weakened them before the agricultural projects got under way. Mother Ann and others went about on preaching tours, and, both at home and abroad, the pacifist Shakers were accused in those revolutionary years of being British spies, as well as blasphemers, and were set upon by angry mobs and irate officials.

Yet the community grew. The tours won some souls, even if at the price of stonings and beatings which undoubtedly shortened the lives of both Mother Ann and her brother. The Shakers reaped a harvest from an upstate revival in 1779, as they did from the Kentucky revivals a couple of decades later. The Shakers followed in the path of revivals, often preaching at camp meetings. Most revival preaching itself, of course, was not oriented toward Shaker beliefs, yet always there were some spirits awakened by evangelism who found thereafter that they could not rest until they had embraced the level of communal and continent perfection that the Believers exemplified. Until her death in 1784, Ann Lee was truly a mother to her struggling yet growing fellowship of heaven, a strong presence among them, full of rich and edifying counsel.

It was not until three years after the passing of Mother Ann that the movement was formally "gathered in society order" and the quiet empire of Shaker communal houses commenced its remarkable cycle of expansion and decline. At its peak, around 1830, Shakerism had some nineteen communities between Maine and Kentucky, each with several hundred members. They were noted for their diligence and legendary cleanliness, their hearty (and often vegetarian) fare, and their practical inventions—for the Shakers can be credited with a number of innovations from the needle with the eye in the middle (now adapted to sewing machines) to the circular saw. Under Mother Ann's motto, "Hands to work and heart to God," these societies outwardly lived lives of labor and peace. Within, however, the Spirit was leading these called-apart "families" in different directions.[7]

The Shakers

The Shaker community can be considered virtually a paradigm of the non-normative religious expression in America, for it represents most of the prevailing characteristics of excursus religion (except that it did not have much diffuse following, though it did have a widespread general cultural influence). We will examine the characteristics of Shakerism relevant to our purpose in terms of Joachim Wach's three forms of religious expression: the theoretical (myth and doctrine), the practical (worship and practices), and the sociological. These characteristics encapsulate basic features of excursus religion generally.

The basic teachings of Shakerism centered on belief in the dual nature of God, incorporating equally both male and female principles. As the former was incarnate in Jesus, so the latter was in Ann Lee. This second incarnation inaugurated a new age of the church in which men and women were absolutely equal (as they were in the communities), and in which humankind was raised much closer to the kingdom of heaven. Shaker elder Frederick Evans wrote:

> The old heavens and earth—united church and state—are fast passing away, dissolving with the fire of spiritual truth. Out of the material of the old, earthly, civil governments, a civil government will arise—is even now arising—in which right, not might, will predominate. It will be purely secular, a genuine republic. Men and women will be citizens. All citizens will be free-holders. They will inherit and possess the land by right of birth. War will cease with the end of the old monarchical, theological earth.... In the new earth sexuality will be used only for reproduction; eating for strength, not gluttony; drinking for thirst, not drunkenness. And property, being the product of honest toil—as those who will not work will not be allowed to eat—will be for the good of all, the young and the old.[8]

That may sound more like nineteenth-century radical socialism than the evangelical piety, but the Shakers, despite the ecstatic pietism of their beginnings, were not fundamentalist sectaries, even as their belief in the second feminine coming of Christ was scarcely orthodox. Shaker thought was far more closely allied to the radical movements of the day, both spiritual and political, than to ordinary pietism.

We are told by one interpreter that the Shakers "do not generally believe in the miraculous birth or divinity of Jesus, but consider that he was divine in the sense of having power to rise above the lower propensities," and it was the "Christ-Spirit" that was manifested in him and Ann Lee. We are told also "they accept the Christian Bible allegorically and literally [sic], and include among Bibles the Koran, Talmud, Zendavesta, and other books sacred to various nations."[9] The progressivist idea of successive spiritual waves spiraling ever upward, manifesting higher and higher levels in early Christianity, Quakerism, and finally Shakerism in the New World, itself so superior to the old, was popular: another Shaker writer says, "Each spiritual wave, in accordance with the laws of accelerated motion, rose above the preceding bearing the masses higher up the altitudes of wisdom"[10]—this and much else in the same vein suggests chiefly the mood of progressive optimism, tinged with scientistic metaphor, widespread in the age of Emerson and Whitman. Add to this the lively and sympathetic interest of many Shakers in such social idealism as that of Robert Owen and in such high-spirited radical movements as the Locofoco Party.

This liberal quality in a religion that had its origins in the Manchester slum's Shaking Quakers is not surprising if we note that ecstatic religion rooted in oppressed groups, like the more recent Pentecostalism, is really very different from the dogmatic style of fundamentalism with which it is often grouped. Pentecostalism is a unique way of experiencing Christianity, whose experiential freshness has often led to doctrinal innovation. In 1916, for example, the Assemblies of God church was split between trinitarians and those who believed in the "oneness" doctrine, which held that baptism should be in the name of Jesus only, who in himself embraced the fullness of God, and who is the only God. But the radicalism of such unusual beliefs, like Jesus' being the only God, and like the Shakers' belief in the dual nature of divinity, may be overlooked, since they do not follow the patterns of ordinary liberalism.

Such beliefs are not obtained in ordinary ways either. While they may be founded on "searching the Scriptures," the ecstatic or pentecostalist divine does not read the Bible deductively or analytically. His Spirit-filled eclecticism may free-associate the most unlikely verses, moods, and current situations into strikingly unusual intuitive patterns of meaning. He moves with agility from luminous verse to subjective feeling or expression of repressed powers to contemporary application, unbounded by dogma.

An ecstatic like Mother Ann may, in one breath, say something which sounds like the simplest biblical literalism, and, in the next breath, something in the nature of a private revelation never before heard on land or sea. The Bible, in such cases, clearly functions as a symbol of that "otherness" for which the speaker is yearning, as well as a vehicle for words by which to internalize the luminous other. The operative factor in the "direct" revelations is not biblicism but inspiration, and inspiration of a sort consonant with the excursus religious experience.

Shaker doctrine was subjectively expansive, setting an inner construction of reality based on a perception of "otherness" derived from visionary experience against the social construction of reality of the "world's people." In this doctrine were symbols of the exaltation of the structurally weak—women, and also weak classes in society. The doctrine, like the practice, made transcendence immediately available through continuing revelation, coming in the successive waves it postulated. In this sense, even though it can be seen as an idealized progressivism, historically conditioned by the industrial revolution, there is an important anti-historicist theme in Shakerism, as in all utopianism and millenarianism. Its eschatology serves to take the communities of Believers out of ordinary time into participation only in the ideal time of transcendence and divine purpose, where Shakers observe as though from elsewhere the follies of the "world." This is characteristic of excursus religion, for it represents a way of moving out of the structure of society, history, and consciousness, through "cave" initiatory experience, to the erection of inner and symbolic bulwarks against outward structures.

As for Shaker worship, it was regarded as a bizarre yet unforgettable and strangely moving experience by all who saw or participated

in it. Nearly all day Sunday and several weekday evenings were given
over to worship, and parts were rehearsed previously. Worship included precision marches a drillmaster would admire. There were
rapid dances to music with odd and shifting African or Indian
rhythms, which sounded peculiar yet gripping to nineteenth-
century ears and anticipated something of the music of the twentieth century. Song after song was sung with the same effect of
mysterious, almost dangerous, beauty. Finally, long periods were
reserved for simple emotional outbursts of praise and "gifts" offered spontaneously, as in the more staid, conventional Quaker
meeting. Gifts of singing and movement were most common, but
there were also gifts of tongues—songs or speeches, sometimes transcribed, in an unknown tongue. Now and again personages, in the
1830s and after, from the spirit world gave messages, and sometimes Shakers received imaginary baskets of fruit and flowers from
the Other Side.

Belief in spirit visitations seemed to grow naturally out of the
primordial Shaker experience of visions and special revelations,
often very graphic in their depiction of paradise. This belief was
certainly enhanced by familiarity with the works of Swedenborg on
the part of informed Shakers like Frederick Evans. It reflects a sense
of the pluralism and complexity of the alternative spiritual world
which is an important feature of excursus religion, and which was to
influence directly its course in America.

The spirits who visited Shakers were mostly biblical characters or
departed Believers. We read such intriguing notes in Shaker memoirs as, "This evening Jacob of old and his twelve sons attended our
meeting," or it might have been Noah or one of the prophets or
Mother Ann or another of the founders. Most remarkable of all, a
record from North Union, Ohio, says, "In the year 1843, when the
Millerites were looking for Christ to come ... he was among the
Shakers spiritually ... He took up his abode at North Union for
the space of three months."[11]

It was in 1837 that a major Spiritualist movement swept through
the Shaker communities. It led to tremendous enthusiasm, uncon-
trolled emotionalism, and highly charged worship services. It is
surprising to realize that it was Spiritualism which led to renewal of
Shaker art and ritual; apparently legitimation by an enraptured

medium was required for the aesthetic side of the Shaker personality to show itself. With Spiritualism came the use of mediums for the testing and proving of members, but also a richer symbolic and aesthetic life. Early Shaker furniture and crafts (which now bring exorbitant prices in antique shops) had the austere beauty of that which is purely functional and honestly made, and whose lines are clean and true. Shaker creations bore no trace of ornament or fanciful twist.

Yet these same masters of plain workmanship, after the spiritual influx of the "Era of the Manifestations," produced a remarkable series of "inspirational drawings," swirling pen or pencil traceries or watercolors showing symbolic maps of heaven or opulent trees of life, all suggesting paradisal vision and the quintessence of aesthetic play. It is noteworthy that these pictures, considered to have sacred meaning within the community and rarely shown to outsiders, originated during the few years of greatest Spiritualist activity but reached their greatest florescence in the decades just after it. There was also, in this other world being opened to mortal eyes and ears, new songs such as that brought by "Mother Ann's little White Dove, November 5, 1843," or by "a little bird which was taken from a spiritual tree that was planted in our meeting room, March 9, 1844."[12]

The new wave also brought rites oddly reminiscent of "cosmic religion." Spring and autumn rituals that included processional singing through the fields and buildings for the blessing of the crops or "cleansing" were initiated. Even more intriguing was the establishment of "Holy Hills of Zion" on Shaker farms. Under inspiration, a hexagonal tract of land would be cleared and fenced, and a "Lord's Stone" bearing a secret inscription set in its center. Here with rapturous singing and dancing and frenzy, twice-yearly "love feasts" were held in the 1840s. They were wholly closed to outsiders, but were times not only of spiritual celebration and offering, but also of meeting with American Indian spirits and the spirit of Mother Ann, whose mysterious "second appearing" was believed to be taking place in the "Era of the Manifestations." Shaker Spiritualism led to many problems and, in the opinion of some, contributed heavily to the decline of the movement. Other nineteenth-century utopian ventures, such as the Rappite and

Owenite communities at New Harmony, Indiana, and the Oneida community, were swept by Spiritualism in their final periods. But it must be emphasized that mid-century Spiritualism, far from being a "decadent" occultism, entwined itself with the optimistic rhetoric of democracy, progress, and the advent of new age. Thus, Frederick Evans, as radical as his fellow-Spiritualist Robert Owen, was quite capable of praising men like Voltaire and Thomas Paine as precursors of the coming just society in which the tyrannies of church and state would be abolished, yet in the same passage contending that Spiritualism was a new influx designed to further that work by converting, through its rappings, moving tables, and so forth, the "scientific Materialists."[13] This last task, the Shakers believed, must be accomplished before the perfect church and social order, foreshadowed by the Shaker communities, can be established here below.

Two fundamental characteristics of excursus religion are evident in Shakerism. One is the reversion to sensorimotor expression. The dances and raptures indicate that when the repressions of structural society—the "world order"—are reversed, a great desire to feel and express oneself physically can be released. This is all the more the case when other symbols of reversal, such as the denial of sexuality, are also operating.

The second characteristic is the influx of symbolic pluralism, in the form of the spirits. This feature is open to debate, for it can also be cogently argued that new religious movements are more monotheistic and more centered on single symbols—a single founder, revelation, rite, place, time—than are established religions. Popular, folk, or even establishment religion inevitably has a certain polycentric quality, symbolized by a diversity of spiritual powers of whatever name: gods, spirits, angels, saints. Mother Lee's movement represents the kind of reaction against this multiverse that often leads to intensive monotheistic or salvation religion focused on single symbols. But the implicit pluralism of the ecstatic style militated against this, as did the open liberalism of many Shakers.

But a more fundamental example of symbolic pluralism is connected with the third of the forms of religious expression, the sociological. After Ann Lee, the basic symbol upon which Shakerism focused, the symbol upon which rested its separateness from

the diffuse environment, was the community itself. With the community in the unifying role, then, other facets of religion were free
to exfoliate. Indeed, exfoliation was necessary. Once the doorway of
community formation had been passed through, Shakerism was a
separate world, loosening more and more ties with the old world,
especially in its subjectivity and in that half of Shaker life of which
outsiders saw but little, the worship. Here, on the other side of the
door, a new world had to be constructed. This new world would
have to be an expression of the ideal, the communitas (in Victor
Turner's term), which the community symbolized. As a symbol of
total communitas, of I-Thou relationships in which all structural
barriers, whether of sex or of life and death, are broken down, it
includes the spirits of the departed and all the powers of the Other
Side. Finally, in the seasonal rites and the consecration of the Holy
Hills, it completes the communitas symbolism to make a new,
sacred cosmos opposite the world's order.

The sacredness of the community is demonstrated by its reversal
of worldly patterns of relation between the sexes and by its members' distinctive dress and speech. As always, though, religious
community is the total of a number of individual processes of
transformation. To each individual in it the community will be the
end of two transitions, first to a certain independence and ego
enhancement when he or she makes the decision to join the community, perhaps at the cost of stormy parting from kindred, and
then of an ego loss, possibly welcome after the great act of self-
affirmation, as identity and personality sink into that of the new
fellowship—which, in the case of a "total institution" like the
Shakers', will construct virtually all of life.

Frederick Evans and Shakerism

Let us look at this passage in the light of the life of one distinguished Shaker, Frederick Evans. He was an agnostic as a young
man, and a radical for most of his life, but lived more than sixty
years in Shakerdom—"on the back side of this world," as he put it.
Evans was born in England in 1808 to middle-class parents. He was
resentful of school and church, and his happiest memories were of
wandering the English fields observing the crops and animals and

talking with the common people. At the age of twelve he was brought to America by his father and brother. The brother, George, better educated than Frederick, became a publisher of radical papers and tracts with titles like *The Workingman's Advocate* and *The Bible of Reason,* in which he urged land reform, equality of men and women in all respects, and abolition of "chattel slavery and wage slavery." George Evans was among the founders of the Locofoco Party in 1835. Reading widely in philosophy and the world religions, but favoring Thomas Paine and Voltaire, Frederick Evans was firmly antagonistic toward "all the wrongs perpetrated by Church and State," and believed in materialism and "Socialistic-Communism." He determined with some friends to form a community based on these principles.

But in 1830, while gathering information on utopian community life, he visited the Shaker house in Mount Lebanon, New York. Expecting a group of fanatics, he was much impressed by "the air of candor and openness"—indeed, after a week, he called them a society of infidels, the highest compliment, he says, of which he was then capable. And his rationalistic antipathy toward past evils wrought in the name of religion only endeared the Shakers to him more, for they had suffered greatly under false and evil religion, and saw in themselves the promise of a better day.

The Shakers prayed for him, and Frederick Evans experienced a spiritual change. It was something so subtle, so strange, that he could hardly put it into words. Only a few seemingly minor signs were enough to suggest to this young confirmed materialist that there was something more than what he had known.

"In one of the first meetings that I attended, I saw a brother exercised in a slight way outwardly; and it gave me the first *evidence* that began to produce in me faith in the *spiritual.*" "One night, soon after retiring, I heard a rustling sound, as of the wind of a flock of doves flying through the window (which was closed) towards my bed; and ... I believed it to be supernatural...." After these tokens, he found he had within him powers, including powers of reason, he had known not of. Visitations of angels came to him at night for about three weeks, and with them a power that moved through his body, starting at the feet. At the end of this, he could not but believe, through his rationality itself, in the existence of a spiritual world, in immortality, in the reality of communication between souls out of the body.

At the same time, he had a strange dream: there was a great fire, and a nude man of perfect physique standing by it. The man stepped into the fire, which encircled his whole body. Next the dreamer observed that, though of perfect beauty, the man was, as Evans delicately put it, "so organically changed that no fig-leaf covering was required."[14]

With such signs on both inner and outer planes, how could he resist the call to join this community at once radical, spiritual, and celibate? He easily convinced himself that the Shakers were the truest of all rationalists, able to defend their beliefs, for they were based on their own experience, and that better than anyone else they put the principles of socialism and reform into practice. So he went from the politics of alienated idealism to an order exemplifying the same ideals almost outside of this world, but in communion with the better realities of the spiritual world.

All of this indicates general characteristics of the sociological expression of excursus religion. The community, because it must bear the burden of being the salient symbol of the oneness and communitas the movement seeks, may be exceptionally close-knit at its core—even a total institution. At the same time, of course, it will have, as did the Shakers, circles of admirers (perhaps in other religions) outside its institution or in peripheral contact with it. It will also have, as did the Shakers, large numbers of "in and out" adherents, for it cannot offer structural inducements to compensate for loss of fervor or weariness with intensely spiritual life. Finally, it will be a community of "core" people who have, ideally, passed through an initiatory transformation of sufficient strength to make them secure in their membership.

The Shakers were far from the only expression of excursus religion and search for communitas to appear in the spiritually restless America of the first half of the nineteenth century. Without speaking of transcendentalist New England or the camp meetings of the frontiers, the spiritual children of Mother Ann Lee had many interesting colleagues in upstate New York, where they first settled. They provide an instructive pattern of variations of the excursus type.

Carl Carmer has pointed out that there stretches a belt scarcely twenty-five miles wide across New York state from east of Albany to Buffalo which invites the wonder of the religious world. He calls it, for the phenomena that took place in it in the first half of the last century, Spirit Way; it is also the "Burned Over District" where sparks lingering from revival fires lit the oil of stranger lamps.[15]

Here was the 1779 revival, an afterglow of the Great Awakening, and here was the Shakers' original Watervliet settlement which increased its numbers as a result of fall-out from that 1779 work of grace. In Spirit Way was also the last settlement of the Jemimakins and the last resting place of the Publick Universal Friend. Here, in 1824, the great evangelist Charles Finney began his ministry of hell-fire preaching and social concern; and here not long after, in 1827, Joseph Smith found the golden plates with their tales of fabulous spiritual adventure in early America. And here it was that, beginning about 1833, William Miller commenced preaching the end of the world and the second coming of Christ on October 22, 1843, and his followers gathered in white robes on hilltops and housetops to await the consummation of the ages and meet the Lord in the air. Out of this movement came indirectly the Seventh-Day Adventist Church.

Here it was also that the Oneida Community, founded by John Humphrey Noyes, flourished from about 1835 to 1885. It offers an interesting contrast to Shakerism. Noyes believed, as the Shakers did, in the present possibility of Christian perfection, and that perfection required that all beings must love each other equally well. But at Oneida this admirable goal did not eventuate in celibacy, but in a system known as Complex Marriage. Through it every member of the community was entitled to have sexual inter-course with any member of the opposite sex, though only under the supervision of a Central Committee. The committee generally ap-proved requests when contraception through retention of the se-men was to be observed, but exercised stricter control over the procreation of future members of the society, in an endeavor to practice scientific eugenics. The one great sin Oneidists were to avoid was "special love"—a particularized sexual or other attach-ment between two members at the expense of equal love for all. Oneida, then, reversed the ordinary "structural" pattern of social

and family life and relations between the sexes as much as did the
Shakers, but in the opposite direction.

Finally, it was within the purlieu of the Spirit Way that, in 1848,
the Fox sisters heard the mysterious rappings which they and many
others took to be messages from departed spirits. That event,
whatever else may be said of it, was exaltation of the structurally
weak, for Margaretta and Catherine Fox were female, aged 15 and
12 respectively, and of a poor rural family. From the Fox sisters
stems the Spiritualist movement. But much else besides this episode must have gone into the explosive Spiritualist enthusiasm of
the 1850s, for the match from Hydesville, New York, struck dry
grass indeed.

Within a year or two of the "Rochester rappings," and the
attendant newspaper stories, there were spirit circles in most major
American cities. In some places, like the Western Reserve section of
Ohio, it was said the regular churches were half deserted for the
conventicles of the new craze. Tales of the Shaker experience account for part of this, and tales of Amerindian shamanism account
for part. But a major factor was an intellectual tradition providing a
structure all fit and ready to be filled by the influx of actual
experience, such as the Fox sisters provided. To that tradition we
must now turn. Rarely has the way been better prepared for an
excursus experience than in this case.

Swedenborg

To understand non-normative spirituality in American history, one
could do much worse than begin in eighteenth-century Sweden
with the remarkable scientist and mystic Emanuel Swedenborg.
Spiritualism, Theosophy, and "New Thought" have all been
deeply influenced in their intellectual constructions by his ideas, or,
rather, by his highly creative reworking and popularization of that
platonic idealism tinged with theurgic mysticism which has ever
been a fountainhead of emergent religions in the West. Both as
source of ideology and as paradigmatic model of the modern man
of initiatory experience, Swedenborg has influenced counterspirituality as has no one since Plato himself.

Born in 1688, Emanuel Swedenborg was the son of a Lutheran

court chaplain and bishop. His father was an outstanding man in his day; strictly pious, he was nonetheless a cleric of broad sympathies, an advocate of church union, and an enthusiastic reformer. Like his more famous son, the bishop had a lively awareness of invisible spiritual realities; he believed firmly in the ministrations of angels among men and declared that from time to time he conversed with his guardian angel.

Emanuel Swedenborg, however, turned to science before he turned to religion. He was appointed to the Swedish Board of Mines, and did significant work in metallurgy and mining engineering. In the manner of his time, though, Swedenborg was by no means a narrow specialist. He proposed a version of the nebular hypothesis of the origin of the solar system many years before Kant, Herschel, or Laplace; his work in anatomy, crystallography, and other fields was comparably in advance of its time, and had less effect on the development of European science than it deserved partly because Sweden was then a land well outside the mainstream of intellectual life.

His searching intellectual interests, though, did not exhaust themselves in such inquiries. He became interested in the problem of the nature of life, and the result was his book *The Economy of the Animal Kingdom* (1740-41; revised as *The Animal Kingdom*, 1744-45—the "animal" of the title is from the Latin *anima*, "soul," so refers to the realm of all things animated by life). In the book, Swedenborg posits that the soul, the principle which sets living matter apart from inert, cannot be located anatomically. The closest one can come to it is in life's energy, in the "tremulations" which characterize organic matter; but the real source of life seems to lie elsewhere. At this stage we may note the use of scientific information and method (at least as a start) in what is really a spiritual quest. But here, and in a book *On the Worship and Love of God*, which he wrote at about the same time, Swedenborg moved from science to reason, then to the use of analogy, and finally to careful intuition, saying the mind can *see* truth, as well as learn it by observation and reason.

All this is typical of the alternative tradition. It represents that side of mysticism which is really closer to science than to historical-revelation religions, or to the community orientation of the temple.

Like science, it views a universe of quiet and eternal truth which must be patiently explored, rather than Sinaitic revelation; and like science it has no high opinion of the verification validity of majority opinions. Indeed, modern science and esotericism have a common background in late medieval and renaissance Rosicrucianism and alchemy.

In 1744-45 Swedenborg passed through an initiation to a new manner of life. Because he kept a remarkable set of diaries of his dreams and visions, the process is not hidden. Late in 1744 the scientist experienced a series of dreams which induced profound humility, for they brought home his sinfulness and his tendency toward intellectual pride. Then, in April of 1745, came a decisive vision in which a man appeared to him while he was eating dinner in an inn; the man later introduced himself to the Swedish seer as none other than the Lord God himself. He told Swedenborg he should write as he was guided about the spiritual meaning of scripture; he was also shown, not for the last time, the realms of spirits, and heaven and hell.

Thereafter Swedenborg was eminently a resident of two worlds. Although he soon retired from his position with the Board of Mines, he traveled widely and was a respected member of the European intellectual community. At the same time, he frequented the other world, where he learned the state of departed spirits, and conversed with the shades of past worthies. Based on these experiences, he wrote heavy tomes of theology and scriptural exposition. So much were these two sides combined in the same man that it was not uncommon, in the midst of some learned conversation, for the Swede to raise eyebrows by commenting, "Yes, I just recently discussed that point with the Apostle Paul," or with Luther or Aristotle.

What were the basic ideas of Swedenborg's mature thought? First, he affirmed that spiritual realities are prior to material; everything visible that exists does so because of a spiritual force. The complexity of the visible world, then, owes to a complexity of the spiritual; things are what they are because of an elaborate system of correspondences between the two realms, an *analogia entis,* to which the key is the scripture understood allegorically. The pivot of the visible realm (as in his earlier nebular hypothesis) is the sun, which reflects God, who is the spiritual sun of the spiritual world. (This is a common motif of ancient and renaissance Neo-platonism.)

We may pause here to note a couple of themes already apparent in Swedenborgianism. First, there is the evident drive to put sacred things in "scientific" form. Swedenborg was looking for a language to express relations between the infinite and the finite which would have mathematical and scientific exactitude; this he found in cor-respondences. Second, there is evident a kind of rationalism or mentalism which makes thought or spirit, independent of space and time, prior to the visible universe and able ideally to know all places and times in all worlds. Both these themes are evident in his spiritual progeny, from William Blake and Ralph Waldo Emerson (both of whom are indebted to the Swedish sage) to Spiritualism, Theosophy, and "New Thought"—with its belief in healing and controlling through proper thinking, and its love of the word "science," as in "science of mind," "Christian Science," and the like.

As a theologian, Swedenborg denied the traditional Trinity but taught that the entirety of God—Father, Son, and Holy Spirit—was in Jesus Christ. The Father is the inmost principle of divinity within Jesus, the Son its manifestation, the Spirit its outward-working energy. (The doctrine can be compared with that of the "oneness" Pentecostalists.) The Spiritual Sun which is God for us shines wholly through the glorious clouds of the human flesh of Jesus Christ; it is to Jesus that Swedenborgian prayers are addressed.

Another unusual Swedenborgian doctrine concerns the Last Judgment—Swedenborg claimed that it had already taken place in 1757, and that he had been allowed to observe it as a representative of the world of humankind. But just as the coming of God in Jesus Christ was not done in exactly the way the Jews expected, so was the Judgment not exactly what conventional Christians expect—and still fruitlessly await, even as Jews still await the Messiah. Instead, the Judgment took place wholly in the spiritual realm, and cleared away certain evil forces to allow the Second Coming in the form of a powerful new spiritual influx. Evolution in the material world cannot come by natural causes, but can only be the result of a new spiritual arrangement and power input, since by the law of correspondences all below reflects its invisible spiritual causes. Sweden-borgians argue that those who reject Swedenborg's account of the Judgment and spiritual Second Coming must be prepared to offer some equally far-reaching explanation of the unprecedented changes in human life and consciousness since around the middle of the eighteenth century.[16]

Swedenborg's notions may at first sound odd. But it is not for nothing that William Blake, who was greatly influenced by the Swede, has joined Nietzsche as a patron saint of recent "radical" and "death of God" theology. For all its queer kabbalism, Swe-denborg's thought can be interpreted not only as a throwback to Neoplatonism, but also as presenting a new "secular Christ" and a new dispensation for "mankind come of age." In his vision of the 1757 Judgment, he saw emblazoned in heaven the words *nunc licet,* "now it is pemitted."

There is a third side to Swedenborg's offering, and that is his accounts of the worlds of departed spirits, based on his numerous journeys to them. These realms, which directly reflect the thoughts of their inmates, have an almost psychedelic splendor, yet are also places of learning, for the sage tells us spirits advance from joy to greater joy there as they grow in wisdom and love. Heaven and hell both exist, but they are states rather than places, and spirits may move from the latter to the former as they are able to abide it—but those of certain temperaments tend to wish each other's company. Higher spirits continually greet and guide novices on the other shore. Whatever one makes of his visions, Swedenborg's spiritual-ism can be said to have a modern ring about it, in that it evidences a "triumph of the therapeutic" over the forensic and punitive con-cepts of the afterlife that prevailed in his day.

But for all that, Swedenborg was also a man of his time. He may have seen heavens of glowing luminosity, but he did not perceive natural beauty in this world. Once, journeying from Florence to Leghorn, he wrote, "the road was fine, *but* there were mountains on both sides." His style of excursus religion had nothing to do with the still-to-come romanticism and romantic concept of beauty; it was, rather, intellectual theosophy indebted to Descartes and Boehme, but not to aesthetics. In art Swedenborg favored only the most direct realism.

All this must have some relationship to the prodigiousness of his verbal expression, the photographic literalness in the presentation of his visions, and his elaborate yet wooden dissertations on religious language and symbol, in which every important term in the Bible is made to have a single, direct, symbolic meaning. The meanings are often provocative, yet they suggest a certain fixation on words found also in the writer's rejection of sacramentalism—on the grounds that only motives, not acts, are saving—and his remarkable affirmation that the Word of God in the Bible *is* God.

Swedenborg was ascetic in many respects. He was virtually vegetarian and rarely drank; he was a lifelong celibate who vowed not to marry after an unhappy love affair as a very young man. But the dreams he records as coming just before his decisive vision in 1745 contain explicit sexual elements, and he was the author of a justly celebrated book on marital love, in which he pointed out that, in contrast to the spirit worlds, where marriages may be consummated and completed, in this life so few marriages really work out on a deep level that we have hardly any idea what "conjugial love" really is or can be. His austere regimen and volcanic inner life were apparently salutary for him; his tall, thin frame crowned by snowy white hair was tough as a willow, and he wrote his most lucid and important book, *The True Christian Religion*, at the advanced age of eighty-three. Of him Jorge Luis Borges wrote:

> Taller than the others, this man
> Walked among them, at a distance,
> Now and then calling the angels
> By their secret names. He would see
> That which earthly eyes do not see:
> The fierce geometry, the crystal
> Labyrinth of God and the sordid
> Milling of infernal delights.
> He knew that Glory and Hell too
> Are in your soul, with all their myths;
> He knew, like the Greek, that the days
> Of time are Eternity's mirrors.
> In dry Latin he went on listing
> The unconditional Last Things.[17]

Johnny Appleseed

John Humphrey Noyes, of the Oneida community, once said that Spiritualism was Swedenborgianism Americanized. While this may be an overstatement, it is far from completely false. Swedenborg's books, popular for their sensational material despite the heavy style and bulk, were well known in the new world.

The ideas contained in them had an important intellectual influence on Emerson; on William and Henry James through their Swedenborgian father; and on other transcendentalists, who, in turn, influenced the "New Thought" movement and Christian Science. The fundamental idea that moves through the latter two, that specific spiritual causes aligned to thought affect material events, was certainly transmitted to the founders of these popular American religions via the Swedish sage. Then there was, and is, the Swedenborgian church in America, properly called the Church of the New Jerusalem (called by its followers the "New Church"), which, though small, goes back to colonial times and has been influential. The church, and literature published by it, made millions vaguely aware of Swedenborgian ideas about spirits, the nature of the afterlife, and judgment. This, in turn, set the stage for Spiritualism, although one should hasten to add that the Swedenborgian Church strongly discourages mediumship, feeling in strong group and grid fashion that its founder's gifts were very exceptional and that the efforts of others to imitate his interworld communication are likely to end in trouble. In the turbulent and adventurous America of the last century, though, such warnings seemed hopelessly stodgy.

One link between Swedenborg and Spiritualism was John Chapman (1774-1845), better known as "Johnny Appleseed." An orphan raised in western Massachusetts, Chapman went to the frontier early, but not before he had come into contact with Swedenborgianism and been converted. Never married, vegetarian, friend of pioneer, Indian, and animal, he was something of a native American saint, and there grew up around him the folk legends suitable to a popular holy man. He carried his appleseed business as far west as Ohio, providing an item of greatest economic importance to the pioneers. But in the frontier cabins he left not only apples, but also Swedenborgian literature, especially chapters of Swedenborg's *Heaven and Hell*. "Good news fresh from heaven!" he called it.[18]

The more recondite elements of the Stockholm philosopher's

work may have eluded the frontiersman, but the graphic accounts of what happens to one's soul after death were his meat. His life was hard, brutal, and deprived. His labor was endless, hunger was never far from the door, and half his children might well die of disease. Many of his communities knew no higher entertainment than drunkenness and brawling. Yet at the same time there was in his breast a free-floating idealism—he was building a new land where the shackles of the old order would have no hold—and he yearned to know, with a definiteness that could withstand relentless Yankee skepticism, the state of his loved ones who had passed over before him.

The new dispensationalism, the gutsy heterodoxy, and the concrete spiritualism of the Swedenborgian tracts left by Johnny Appleseed had their appeal for the pioneers. The New Church as an institution did not particularly flourish on the frontier, but many a lonely evening must have been spent around cabin fires talking about whether it was true that souls on the other side gather in communities according to temperament, or whether truly conjugal husbands and wives are reunited for eternity. When the new Spiritualism with its mediumship and churches came along in the 1850s, it is no wonder that the areas Johnny Appleseed had worked most assiduously, such as the Western Reserve region of Ohio, turned eagerly, if temporarily, to the new faith, leaving conventional churches half empty.

Mesmerism

Another European influence joined with Swedenborgianism in fermenting the yeasty American brew that led to Spiritualism. That was the teaching and work of Franz Anton Mesmer (1734–1815), the father of modern "Mesmerism" or hypnotism. Mesmerism was concerned with psychosomatic medicine and psychotherapy, and also with a more speculative philosophy about "animal magnetism," which sought to interpret Mesmer's uncanny-seeming discoveries. Underlying these teachings was Mesmer's doctrine of a subtle, universal substance which gives life and vitality; sickness is due to its loss or imbalance. At first Mesmer sought to regulate its influx by magnets, but later discovered that it could be transmitted by persons even better through a process called "animal magnetism." The techniques varied; there was stroking, suggestion, and the famous seancelike sessions in which several patients sat around a vat of dilute sulfuric acid while holding hands or iron bars in contact with the chemical. In any case, the treatment was easily capable of producing hypnotic trance-states which could measurably aid in a cure if the ailment was psychosomatic or psychiatric.

It was a short step for the next generation of savants to take matters further in two directions: scientists like Braid, Charcot, and Freud developed from Mesmer's work, and from other sources, medical hypnosis and psychoanalytic ideas of the unconscious; those of more occult bent sought out the cosmically cognitive meaning of the mesmeric state and the paranormal potential of the powers involved in Mesmerism.

Mesmer did nothing to discourage the second option. In his *Memoir* of 1799, he presents as scientific fact the power of animal magnetism to awaken latent powers that enable people to penetrate universal mysteries, to experience extrasensory perception and precognition, and to heal. He states that it releases an inner sense and power, available also in somnambulism, to which all time and space is one; with it one may see past, present, and future, and to it the secrets of dreams, diagnosis, and philosophy are unveiled. Mesmer felt that much of the work of sibyls, oracles, alchemists, mystics, and occultists of the past was valid, though for reasons that had previously not been understood. It was on this basis that Madame Blavatsky later praised Mesmer enthusiastically, calling Mesmerism the most important branch of magic, and, indeed, the true base of what is called magical or miraculous.[19]

This is the Mesmerism which, especially as it was a subject of experimentation by all sorts of enthusiasts in the New World with more curiosity than caution, helped turn Swedenborgian doctrine and Transcendental mysticism into Spiritualism and Theosophy.

New England Transcendentalism

Another movement which, in convergence with Swedenborgianism and Mesmerism, had a far-reaching impact on the American emergent spiritual tradition and helped effect the thorough American-

ization of those imports was New England Transcendentalism. This
name is primarily associated with a group of thinkers who lived in
and around Boston in the 1830s and 1840s, including Ralph Waldo
Emerson, Amos Bronson Alcott, Orestes Brownson, James Freeman
Clarke, and Henry Thoreau. They contributed substantially to the
appearance of later movements such as Spiritualism, Theosophy,
and Western Zen in several ways: through their establishment of an
American style of contemplative and mystical thought rooted in
metaphysics of the Platonic, Swedenborgian, and Indic sort; through
their popularization of Eastern religious philosophy; through their
example—in this respect Thoreau at Walden and the Brook Farm
communal experiment were especially significant—of an American idealistic "drop-out" life-style which was intellectually and
socially an important statement.

Catherine L. Albanese has shown in a provocative study that the
basic idea of the Transcendentalists was the ancient concept of
correspondences, derived partly from Neoplatonism through Swedenborg.[20] (The latter's works were very widely read and discussed
in American intellectual circles in the 1830s.) The universe was
structurally identical with the human form, and its meaning was
embedded, had one eyes to see, in every segment of it. All this
meant that the cosmos was harmonious and fundamentally benign.
Transcendentalism has evolved from Calvinism through Unitari-
anism, laying aside the sterner doctrines of the older orthodoxies,
but preserving a sense of intrinsic laws in the universe and the
Puritan's moral earnestness in a far more open and impersonal
cosmos. It was an ideology for the intellectual elect of the era of
Jacksonian democracy, of the rapid expansion of the frontier, of
seemingly unlimited opportunity, and of the worldwide contacts
effected by Yankee traders.

But in a deeper sense Transcendentalism was conservative, even
as was Gnosticism and European occultism before it, and Spiritualism, Theosophy, and Western Zen subsequently. Like them it
sought, in a remoter past than the immediate, intellectual supports
for understanding what was palpably a new day of the Spirit. To
interpret, and find spiritual ways of living with, the new fact which
was democratic and progressive America—an America intoxicated
with the ideas of change, expansion, and a brighter tomorrow—

Transcendentalists looked not to Calvinism, Lockeanism, Deism, the nation's direct intellectual antecedents. It searched out instead subtler and more ancient doctrines which could give even wider meaning to the new experience: the divine in all persons, the universe in all its parts, timeless motifs enacted in the historical dramas of the present, intuition rather than reason the tool for confronting events and key to the universe, contemplative retirement the mainspring of truly significant action.

For example, Albanese speaks of the "kinetic revolution" in Transcendentalist thought. Its glorification of movement and change obviously reflects the current frontier situation, but motion typically becomes for those thinkers a universal absolute. Emerson repeatedly speaks of rest as decay, of motion as a form of perfection, of challenges to leave the shore and plunge into the Unlimited and the Immensities. But this absolutizing of movement itself as a basically spiritual, cosmic thing obviates the concrete historical importance of particular movement, such as the westward expansion of the frontier. As historians the Transcendentalists were, in fact, antihistorians: for them history had a unique meaning for each person, as a project for learning one's own cosmic identity; on the other hand, a person could learn all history of true significance for himself from out of the depths of his own consciousness.

The genuine heirs of the Transcendentalist movement, then, were not the practical-minded pioneers, but those for whom movement itself was a spiritual symbol, a token of liminality and transcendence. Those were travelers in the excursus tradition who literally and significantly acted it out, like Mother Ann and The Publick Universal Friend and "Johnny Appleseed," and, as we shall see, the early Theosophists en route to India, and the later Zen "Beats" going "on the road" or living the life of "Dharma Bums."

New England Transcendentalism was not explicitly religious. Thoreau said he would rather hear cowbells than church bells on Sunday morning. But it has nourished religions and quasi-religions. More than that, one does not hesitate to say that, because of the impeccable intellectual credentials of its principal thinkers, it has done more than any other force to legitimate in America the whole bundle of alternative spiritualities which have come to these shores, and to present paradigms for their domestication.

Andrew Jackson Davis

An important source for Spiritualist thought was Andrew Jackson
Davis (1826–1910), the "Poughkeepsie seer," a prolific writer whose
work was supposed to have been initiated in part by the shade of
Swedenborg. Davis is a classic example of a person of indifferent
background who, after a remarkable initiatory experience, found a
place for himself in the emergent tradition and became a mouth-
piece for radical religion.

Davis's parents were uneducated and poor; his father was a
coarse, hard-drinking drifter who continually berated his son for
the boy's lack of "manliness." Despite a miserable childhood,
Davis did manage to learn some letters at a Lancastrian school. At
sixteen, he left home to become apprenticed to the keeper of a shoe
shop in Poughkeepsie, New York.

In the 1840's, Mesmerism and Swedenborgianism were both
popular in America; they were widely discussed and written about,
and the former was widely practiced by amateurs and professionals
alike. Davis, while still in his teens, combined the two. In Poughkeepsie he fell in with a circle which practiced Mesmerism, and was
reportedly an adept study, quickly developing remarkable powers
of clairvoyance, medical diagnosis, and mystic vision while in hypnotic trance. Soon he left the shoe shop to support himself as a
trance healer and stage hypnotist.

A few months after he began the Mesmerism experiments, when
he was seventeen, came Davis's major mystical experiences. This
was also shortly after his mother, to whom he had been closer than
to anyone else, had been delivered from her hard lot by death.
Davis was awakened one night by his mother's voice, and he went
downstairs. Then, apparently in astral travel, he journeyed through
icy mountains and over deep valleys. He saw a flock of sheep in
great confusion; he helped the shepherd to bring them into order.
Then three figures appeared to him with messages.

First an old Quaker presented a scroll bearing the cryptic words:

> As they were, so they are
> As they are, so they will be!

Then appeared the celebrated physician of antiquity, Galen, who
gave Davis a marvelous staff of healing. Next appeared the tall,

cerebral figure of Swedenborg, who pronounced Davis "an appropriate vessel for the influx and perception of truth and wisdom." Davis sought to leave and return to Poughkeepsie, and at the last minute Galen withheld the staff, saying that before he took it the novice would have to learn to keep an even mind.

But a few days later, after a long Mesmeric session, Davis retired with an odd feeling he had forgotten or lost something. Suddenly in his dark room he saw glowing the rod of Galen and a translucent sheet with these words emblazoned on it: "BEHOLD! Here is thy Magic Staff. Under all circumstances Keep an Even Mind. Take it, Try it, Walk with it, Talk with it, Lean on it, Believe on it Forever." From then on this mysterious cane made up of diamond segments, visible only to mystic eyes, was the adept's joy and reliance.[22]

Shortly after his mystical experiences, Davis announced that he would begin dictating out of trance a series of revelations on philosophical matters. His amanuensis was a Universalist minister named William Fishbough. (It should be noted in passing that clergymen of this denomination were commonly involved in early Spiritualism.) The seances at which these deliverances were given were usually attended by a small circle, which from time to time included Edgar Allan Poe, the Fourierist Albert Brisbane, and Thomas Lake Harris, of whom more later.

The result of these trance revelations was Davis's great work, *The Principles of Nature, Her Divine Revelation and a Voice to Mankind*, published in 1847. Despite its nearly 800 pages, this book spoken by an author of only twenty years and claiming divine inspiration created a sensation. It covers many subjects, including the creation of the world from "liquid fire," the origin of the solar system, and the geological history of the earth. It presents a summary of ancient history from a deistic perspective, showing no special favor to Christianity. There are favorable discussions of Swedenborg and Charles Fourier. Accounts of the spiritual constitution of humankind and of the seven spiritual worlds around earth show how the soul evolves after death. Finally comes a denunciation of the sins of society, including those of clergymen, and an appeal for the creation of a Fourierist utopia.

The book, widely read between 1847 and 1876, was praised and attacked vociferously. The questions of its authenticity as revela-

tion, and of how so young a man of such unprepossessing background came by such learning, was discussed avidly then as later.
That complicated issue cannot be resolved here. While there is little
that is truly original in the work, and long passages are no more
than paraphrases of Robert Chambers's *Vestiges of Creation*, of
Swedenborg, and of Fourierist writings; and while the scribe Fishbough was (as his articles in various journals indicate), a man of
some learning who could have contributed more than he allowed to
the project, there is a certain quality to the *Divine Revelations*
which is fresh and which sets the tone of early Spiritualism. For
Davis, as his many subsequent books reveal, was a writer of vigor
and intelligence, despite a tendency to prolixity. What strikes one
most forcefully in the *Divine Revelations* is the unbounded optimism, the exuberant belief in progress in both this world and the
next, the radical and youthful confidence that history is turning
under spiritual influx and that the evils of the past are, for the most
part, behind us—an enthusiasm in tune with the mood of the
young nation at that juncture, and met already among the Shakers.
But Davis shared neither the Shakers' Christian piety (to the end of
his long life, he denied that Spiritualism or he himself were Christian), nor Swedenborg's Age of Reason restraint; his was a romantic
and free futurism full of faith in worlds without end.

Davis's own future was fabulous enough. The year following
the publication of his book, the handsome young celebrity had
—following her sensational divorce scandal—married Catherine
DeWolfe, a lady twenty years older than he and of very considerable wealth. (The father of his bride, said to have once been the
second richest man in the country, had made his fortune as a slave
dealer and privateer, a matter which gave the daughter some spiritual uneasiness.) The union of the democratic idealist and the child
of fortune was not to last long, however, for she was called to a
higher sphere in only five years. The widower's inheritance was long
tied up in litigation and, when finally released, soon lost in unfor-
tunate business ventures.

The career of Andrew Jackson Davis can be compared to that of
his contemporary, the incredible D. D. Home (1833-86). Born in
Scotland, Home was raised in America. Like Davis, he enjoyed his
major psychic opening at seventeen, a few months after the death

of his mother, when he heard her voice calling to him from the Other Shore. He caused a sensation in New England and New York in the fifties with his "physical mediumship" and spirit materializations. He went to Europe, where his charm and tales of the remarkable phenomena that attended him gained him entry into the highest circles. He was a favorite of the French Emperor and his glittering court; in England he was the subject of a sensational extortion trial involving a rich and dotty elderly lady who had given him a great amount of money; in Russia he managed to marry successively not one but two ladies of rank and riches, and the czar himself stood as godfather to one of his children. His amazing feats of levitation, of moving tables by non-physical means, of evoking spirit hands and music and the like, were much studied and never proven fraudulent.[22]

The Spiritualist Movement

Swedenborgianism, spread by Johnny Appleseed and others less colorful, rumors of strange goings-on within Shakerdom, and Andrew Jackson Davis's celebrated book—all were kindling for the fire of Spiritualism and helped to make it not just a book-philosophy or an esoteric experience reserved for the few but a new adventure for the masses. It needed only a spark, a paradigmatic event demonstrating that, for anyone, however humble, the spirit world was real; and that even now, in our day, that world was contacting us. The spark was provided by the "Rochester rappings." The Fox sisters, who heard the rappings, were hardly mighty savants like the Swede, nor even native initiates like Davis and Home, but plain farmgirls of no great education or wit; precisely because of that, when they began communicating with some entity in their house through taps not unlike Morse Code and publicized the phenomena, they joined the number of those through whom emergent religion has surfaced into popular culture.

Spiritualism was, in fact, more of a popular culture movement than a religious movement in a strictly ecclesiastical sense; like excursus religion generally, it avoided direct competition with structural institutions by being either looser or tighter than they, and usually looser. It was not until the last quarter of the century

that Spiritualist churches and national denominations were formed;
then as now, these were not overly successful and accounted for only
a fraction of the diffuse public interest in mediumship and other
Spiritualist phenomena. During the 1850s, when Spiritualist enthusiasm reached its high point, the movement was a disorganized
but effervescent world of "home circles" practicing amateur
mediumship and table-tilting, of famous lecturers and performers,
of numerous Spiritualist books and magazines. Sensational stories
in the newspapers of Spiritualist scandal and success whetted the
public appetite for more. Experimental communal groups, like
Brook Farm, Hopedale, Ceresco, and New Harmony, as well as new
Spiritualist utopias like Mountain Cove and Kiantone, followed the
Shakers in reporting Spiritualist phenomena—a social process also
noted in many of the experimental communes of the 1960s, as
groups grew more and more into themselves as total institutions
separate from ordinary society.

Typical of American Spiritualism in the 1850s was the "Spirit
Room" of the Koons family in their remote farm in southeast
Ohio. In 1852 the head of the household, Jonathan Koons, an
erstwhile freethinker, investigated Spiritualism and found himself
an effective medium. The Spirit Room, actually a detached log
cabin, was built according to spirit specifications, and was inhabited
by a band of one hundred sixty-five high spirits, who manifested
themselves in seances attracting neighbors from miles around and,
in time, visitors from distant states. Not only did this merry band
deliver messages glibly through two tin horns, but would take up
drums, fiddles, horns, and other instruments in the darkened room
to produce a spiritual shivaree audible for more than a mile. The
seance would culminate in the appearance of a luminous spirit hand,
detached at the wrist, which would rapidly write messages on sheets
of paper. The experience of transcendence in American Spiritualism
was by no means always solemn; once when a curious investigator
placed his face too close to the writing spirit-hand, the revenant
mischievously poked his nose with the dull end of the pencil.[23]

We can note several points about Spiritualism as emergent religion. First, its essential conceptual ideology was hardly new in the
pivotal year 1848 when the Fox girls heard the rappings, but can be
traced back in an almost infinite regress to Davis, Swedenborg,

renaissance and ancient Neoplatonism, and finally, no doubt, to archaic shamanism. It is important to note that 1848 really was of little significance to its *conceptual* evolution, but only to its rise and decline as a specific social manifestation.

Second, we may note that what lifts this tradition out of conceptual philosophy is the appearance of phenomena, chiefly initiatory, in the shamanistic pattern, as evidenced by the call and careers of men like Swedenborg, Davis, and Home. These men recall the magus of antiquity and suggest the revival of paradigmatically shamanistic careers, complete with spiritual call, inner initiation, marvelous flight, journeys to and commerce with other worlds.

Third, through a "structurally weak" person and situation is achieved a moment of symbolic transcendence into the cosmos of the emerging world view—as, for example, in the Fox sisters' experience. The structural weakness and noncompetitive character of the new experience legitimates it as a form of excursus for everyone.

Fourth, we may see that Spiritualism does not form a single monolithic ecclesiastical structure, but a diversity of institutions, some very diffuse and some total—though still ephemeral. Related to this is Spiritualism's connection with progressive idealism; both as an experience close to entertainment, and as a liberal eschatology, Spiritualism had no strong need for institutionalization. This suited well its character as the following of charismatic, shamanistic figures, and as the interpretation of intense and visionary but irregular subjective experiences—not to mention the ample temptations to fraud and egomania which attempts to routinize Spiritualism always afford.

Transformations of Spiritualism

As one would expect of a movement of this sort, Spiritualism went through several stages of development, or more accurately, produced individuals who, initially awakened to commerce with other worlds through Spiritualism, went on to alternative means of realizing spiritual reality and the hope of a new spiritual age. Whitney Cross has noted that few remained active Spiritualists for very long, but that Spiritualism was frequently a step on the road to some form of religious modernism. Spiritualism's scientific language, social awareness, criticism of the Bible and the historical churches, and its speculative mood "must have tended to obliterate any remnants of literal-mindedness and orthodoxy embedded in its converts."[24]

A good example would be Thomas Lake Harris (1823–1906). Harris was a man of elaborate inner life who started his career as a Universalist minister, and who was finally to achieve a measure of fame as the founder and ruler of the Fountain Grove utopian community in California. He was close to Andrew Jackson Davis in the 1840s, around the time of the production of the *Divine Revelations,* and was much under the medium's influence. But he broke with Davis, and thereafter became a Swedenborgian minister. At the same time, his spiritual life was becoming tumultous; he was preoccupied with his inner states and from time to time would fall into deep and uncontrollable trances.

In 1854 Harris had a mystical experience, obviously inspired partly by Swedenborgianism and Spiritualism, of a "counterpartal marriage" to a "Queen Lily of the Conjugial Angels." (The spelling "conjugial" is Swedenborgian.) He believed that a spiritual being of the opposite sex is "counterpart" to each human, and that marriage between the two is basic to the fulfillment of spiritual life. His mystical nuptials were, in fact, a second birth which gave him a new name and a new mission; he declared it was the first of seven steps to his attainment of immortality and deity. After the event, he was freed of his interior obsessions and pathological trances and lived in communion and "conjugial bliss" with his spirit-bride in his nightly dreams; in sleep he was in heaven. This dual life continued the rest of his days; even after he was married to a wife of flesh he remained celibate, having sexual relations only with the spiritual consort, whose prior rights the earthly partner was willing to concede. The other world was rich and alive for Harris; he was also able to see the fairies or "fays" who animated natural objects and even the human body. In this awareness he anticipated both Theosophy and an aspect of the "Neo-Pagan" movements of the twentieth century.

It was sexual mysticism that most stirred Harris, however. Like the Shakers and the kabbala, he taught that the divine has two coequal sides: the Eternal Masculine was divine love, the Eternal Feminine was divine truth, and their union, reflected in human and spiritual conjugial love, was divine ability. Sex possessed him even in his most spiritual moments. Affirming the spiritual significance of the religions of India and elsewhere, he said that the cross as a symbol of God was a lingam lifted to heaven.

His ideas became too heretical for the Swedenborgians, and he left that denomination to make his own way in several utopian communities, leading up to Fountain Grove. At Mountain Cove he was one of the directing mediums. In the end he came to certain ideas paralleling Theosophy: esoteric masters, a spirit world or "luminous kingdom," a sevenfold spiritual path, and a set of cycles or "rounds" of human spiritual evolution. He believed also in a subtle spiritual body which could be energized by practice involving breath and massage—these ideas, doubtless related to the sexual concern, show a characteristic entry into proximity sensory awareness, as does sexual mysticism itself.[25]

Harris was also a trance poet who delivered a vast amount of visionary and didactic verse, metered and rhymed, while in a sleeplike state. While not of the caliber of the work of his main spirit controls in this sphere, Petrarch and Dante, considered as extemporaneous verse it is impressive. Howard Kerr has compared the clairvoyant literary production of people like Harris and Davis to Walt Whitman's "self-dramatization as inspired bard unconstrained by barriers of space or time."[26]

Thus we find Harris, beginning in Spiritualism and Swedenborgianism, finding through it (as did the Shakers) a secondary world which offered sexual sublimation, a wellspring of creativity, a return to proximity senses, an effervescence which enhanced the life of withdrawal communities by placing them, as it were, in an alternative cosmos, and finally (as did the Theosophists and others) finding that alternative cosmos underlying our world, whose wise powers and evolutions explain this tangible sphere.

That was also to be the journey of another man, Henry Steel Olcott. In the early 1870s, the lonely farm of the Eddy brothers in Vermont was a spiritualist magnet comparable, in that respect, to the Koons farm twenty years earlier. Olcott, a lawyer and sometime writer for the *New York Daily Graphic,* visited the scene to write a series of articles, later published as a book, *People from the Other World*. It bespeaks the declining interest in Spiritualism that this fascinating book did not sell well, but, nonetheless, it is important in the story of excursus spirituality in America, for it is not only very revealing of the nineteenth-century Spiritualist experience, with its vivid illustrations of apparitions, but also marks a certain juncture.

Many of the Eddy manifestations were Native American spirits with names like Honto, Daybreak, and Santum; this underscores the importance of the American Indian theme in Spiritualism. "Indian guides" were and are common; descriptions of Native American shamanistic performances, reported by writers like Henry Schoolcraft and William Howitt, were widely read in the days of early Spiritualism, and there was interest in contemporary Native Americans of psychic power like the "Shawnee Prophet" (1768–1837), brother of Chief Tecumseh and a legendary seer. Olcott tells us also of a medium named Elizabeth Compton, of Havana, New York, whose "maternal grandmother, an Indian squaw, was brought up among the whites, but was not unfamiliar with the rude sorceries that prevailed among her people."[27]

What was of most significance about the Eddy phenomena, though, was its role in the final transformation of a part of what was awakened by Spiritualism from American Indians to India. For it was at the Eddy home that Henry Steel Olcott met the enigmatic Madame Blavatsky.

5

Colonel Olcott and Madame Blavatsky Journey to the East

A Fateful Meeting

The history of emergent spirituality is replete with obscure and seemingly happenstance events which have been the conduits through which one cycle of its expression has merged into another. Were these moments not perceived and understood, the emergent tradition would appear not as a tradition, but as isolated excursi. Consider, for example, Andrew Jackson Davis's meeting a group of Mesmerists; young Alan Watts's discovery of a certain bookstore in London which, through a Theosophist, led to Eastern contacts; Jack Kerouac's argument with Neal Cassady about reincarnation; and, perhaps most striking of all, the meeting of Henry Steel Olcott and Helena Blavatsky at a farmhouse near Chittenden, Vermont, where manifestations of the frontier Spiritualist genre were occurring. It is quite possible, however, that this was not a chance meeting, that Blavatsky had traveled to Vermont with the express purpose of encountering Olcott, a lawyer and writer, whose newspaper stories on Spiritualism had attracted attention in New York.

The meeting was on September 17, 1874, after dinner. Olcott had been struck by the fascinating appearance of this Russian woman, with her massive face and scarlet Garibaldian blouse, and when she went outside to roll herself a cigarette, he offered, in the French he had heard her speaking with a companion, to light it for her.

From that moment on Olcott found himself brought into a new world of deeper and deeper wonder. After her arrival at Chittenden, the American Indian guides and innocent little girl spirits who

had manifested themselves there were supplemented by exotic
figures from Russia and Caucasia, regions presumably unfamiliar to
any present except the mysterious madame. These visitants were the
forerunners of a spiritual excursus which would make Spiritualism
itself look tame and provincial.

When Olcott and Blavatsky renewed their acquaintance shortly
afterward in New York, the American was privileged to observe
further examples of his friend's power, from the materialization of
a white butterfly to the production of "real" apparitions at the
seance of a fraudulent medium—much to the latter's fright! As
time went on, Blavatsky gradually introduced Olcott to new concepts about spiritualism and the "phenomena" as well. He learned
that actual, discrete spirits were not usually involved, but instead
"elementals," which the strange lady could control by her "mayavic" power, that is, her ability to manipulate the realm of appearances and the finite entities ensnared in it. She was an adept of
"Eastern Spiritualism" or "Brahma Vidya," which is based on a
deeper science than the crude American Spiritualism and produces
its works through something similar to Mesmerism.

His attention directed to the East, Olcott learned still more: that
there exists an Occult Brotherhood of Eastern Adepts, who live and
operate on both this and higher, more invisible, planes, and who
give instruction to elect disciples on the earthly plane. The "East"
to which they pertain seems almost more a state of mind than a
geographical direction, for Masters are found at the hearts of all
ancient cultures, from the Greek and Egyptian to the Japanese and
the Central American Mayan. However, as we shall see, those
concerned with these cultures came to be most interested in India,
and beyond it, mysterious Tibet. Olcott, under Madame Blavatsky's guidance, started as a student of the African (Egyptian)
Section of the Occult Brotherhood, but was later transferred to the
Indian.

It is with that transfer and with its manifestation, so to speak, in
the journey of Olcott and Blavatsky to India in 1879 that we shall
focus our attention in this chapter. We shall examine the Theosophical movement in America by taking just one facet of that story
and exploring it in some depth. That facet will be the emergence of
the East as a powerful symbol of an alternative spiritual center, a

development not limited to Theosophy but early and paradigmatically expressed in it, and of immense consequence for the
subsequent development of excursus religion.

To understand fully the Theosophical founders' journey to India,
though, requires examining the meaning of their lives in more
detail both before and after the meeting at Chittenden. We shall
do that first in terms of the categories of liminality and communitas
suggested by Victor Turner. For if liminality burgeoning into communitas was manifest as they landed on the Bombay dock, as we
shall see, the seeds which there came to full flower must have been
planted long before.

Liminality and the Theosophical Twins

In chapter 2, we noted that liminality is fundamentally a process
state, a state of transition. Literally or figuratively, one has to travel
out of what is familiar, indeed, from all landmarks whatsoever, in
order to get somewhere new. But for some, as we have seen,
transition can become a permanent state, and liminality a permanent vocation. This is the classic role of the monk, the wandering
friar, holy man, or shaman—or the clown, court jester, or hobo.
The sacred misfit is often a harbinger of cleavage in the social fabric
and of a reversal of the values of ordinary structures. This role is
often reified by such signs as continual wandering or pilgrimage,
celibacy or other non-ordinary sexual and family arrangements,
living with economic instability, even skirting the edge of madness.
In recompense, the permanently liminal person seems to be able to
peer further into invisible reality than those circumscribed by structure—as does the initiate in his night of transition. (Theosophy sees
life as a series of initiations, and the permanently liminal state of
Blavatsky and Olcott seems to express this value to an intense
degree.) Thus the "misfit" friar, shaman, or clown manifests symbolically the continuing possibility of liminality, even as do festival
recapitulations of return to chaos and renewal for those who only
enter liminality periodically and ritually.

Olcott and Blavatsky, the "Theosophical Twins" as Olcott liked
to call them, richly exemplified this liminal wandering vocation in
their voyage to India. All her life, Helena Petrovna Blavatsky

(1831–91) personified the vocation of permanently dwelling in or near liminality. With her exotic accent, hints of an adventurous past, imported cigarettes, rough-edged tongue, amazing psychic phenomena, and aura of being an envoy of mysterious powers, she was always a wanderer, a colorful misfit in whatever society she found herself. She spoke, like a magus of old, of having received occult initiations in the East and of wandering to arcane shrines of wisdom. She originally came to America in 1873, she said, because it was the birthplace of Spiritualism, and she was drawn to it as "a Mohammedan approaching the birthplace of his prophet." She confessed in 1874 that, "For the sake of Spiritualism I have left my home, an easy life amongst a civilized society, and have become a wanderer upon the face of this earth."[1] As we have seen, though, behind her interest in Spiritualism lay an interest in deeper mysteries and in the East. Olcott shared this interest, and to him fell the task of creating in Theosophy new forms of social structure to mediate the wisdom of the other world he had touched.

Both Blavatsky and Olcott had backgrounds of status within the established social structure, as different as those backgrounds were. The Russian lady was born the daughter of an officer and granddaughter of a provincial governor of the Czar. Henry Steel Olcott was born of successful American farmers and rose to reasonable success and recognition in several fields. Neither of the future Theosophists, however, found their status satisfactory.

Helena Blavatsky

Helena, who grew up on vast estates near the Volga, was a difficult and unmanageable child. She would hide for hours, or tell long and fantastic stories about the lives and past lives of the mounted animals in her grandfather's museum. As an adolescent she once deliberately scalded her foot in boiling water so she would not have to go to a viceroy's ball. At sixteen she married N. V. Blavatsky, a widower in his forties, who served as vice-governor of Erivan in Armenia. Helena made her typically impulsive decision on the rebound from a disappointed infatuation, apparently in response to taunts that no man would have such an odd young lady.

But the ill-matched couple did not stay together for long. The future chronicler of the cosmic pilgrim left Russia and began her restless wanderings. Differing accounts are given of these years, but it is evident that they included the development of exceptional psychic and mediumistic skills and a corresponding fascination with occult lore and the wonder-workers of the earth. Blavatsky's way of life undoubtedly reflected how she felt about herself: marginal to normative society, without important external bonds, but possessed of a deeply felt and complex subjectivity.

Somehow during this time the grip of ordinary life grew weaker and weaker, and the gates of access to deeper alternative realities wider. It was a process comparable to that through which Swedenborg was vouchsafed his visions of the Other Side, the Shakers discovered their spirit paradises, and Thomas Lake Harris found his way to the bower of his immortal bride. In the case of Madame Blavatsky, the steps of the process are less clear, the end result possibly even more self-transformative. Perhaps it began in 1851, after the break-up of her marriage, when her father took her to London, where she reported seeing a princely, turbaned man she said would ever after be her Master. He was with a delegation of Indian and Nepali princes in the British capital at the time.

Except for the period between 1858 and 1864, when she was back in Russia with her family and, for a time, with her husband, amazing her social circle with psychic phenomena, not much is known of her life between 1851 and 1871.

These years were certainly spent in restless travel. She was apparently with Garibaldi's forces at the battle of Mentana in 1867. But according to her account, she traveled further afield, crossing America in a covered wagon, and finally reached India and Tibet, where she received initiations from her Masters.

The memoirs of her cousin, Count S. Y. Witte (1849–1915), distinguished statesman and prime minister of Russia 1905–6, and other accounts, paint rather a different picture of those years. They tell of her wandering about Europe with an opera singer, impulsively dabbling in radicalism, and engaging in such varied enterprises as riding horses in a Turkish circus and managing the Servian royal choir. But Witte's testimony is weakened by the fact that it was written more than fifty years after events that would have occurred when he was only a child or teen-ager. On the other hand,

it can be presumed to represent family tradition about the notorious relative.

Helena Blavatsky's own accounts of those years contain incon-
sistencies, not to mention improbabilities, even as her psychic
phenomena undoubtedly employed some illusion. And her writing
is replete with examples of unattributed borrowing, though perhaps not as many as some critics have supposed. [2]

It is not our primary task, however, to explore, much less to
judge, these matters here. We are instead concerned with the
overall significance, especially on the symbolic level, of Theosophy
in American spiritual history, rather than with a detailed or critical
biography of the Russian woman.

In light of her symbolic role, even her beguilements can be
grasped. Whether one condones them or not, they are of a nature
which, in the context of her life and teaching, identify her with
archetypal figures from myth and religious typology: the trickster
(as we have seen), the shaman, the magus. But love of trickery in
this nineteenth-century parlor shaman led her more than once into
foolishness and embarrassing situations, and came close to dis-
crediting her cause completely.

Yet that it did not for many followers both Eastern and Western,
and that her movement finally came to have a certain influence, can
only be attributed to the likelihood that her particular style of
trickery was so consistent with her role as magus as to be unper-
ceived as trickery. Or, if it was so perceived, it was taken only to
reinforce the archetype, as being a kind of trickery legitimate to the
shaman or magus, if not essential to her social and spiritual role.
One gets a feeling that Olcott, who never conceded trickery on his
companion's part but who sometimes seems to leave that interpretation open to all but the most credulous readers of his memoirs,
probably understood some of her ''phenomena'' in that light. That
interpretation would, of course, apply only to those who were, so to
speak, in the magus's world; for the many critics outside it, it is
only trickery, or at best raw psychic power without significance, as
are the miracles of all religions to nonbelievers.

Three ways in which this trickery can be related to Madame
Blavatsky's vocation come to mind. First, she was like a shaman,
with her preternatural guides, and shamans commonly employ

both sleight-of-hand and inflated narratives about their own supernatural initiations to facilitate belief and confidence in their clients.
Second, she was, as we have seen, like a trickster in that she enjoyed
fooling people and thereby deflating the pretensions of society, a
labor congenial to the genuine outsider and denizen of two worlds
—the trickster is at once righteous, comic, and amoral. Third, the
evidence suggests she may have had at least a mild case of dissocia-
tion or multiple personality, a condition in which each personality
may operate by quite different values and have different goals from
the others, and may not even be aware of everything the other does.
While pathological if extreme, some degree of multiple personality
may comport with many important religious phenomena: visions,
possessions, and inspiration. When one learns how to "trigger" the
shift, even while attributing it to supernatural overshadowing, it
facilitates mediumship and shamanism. Some capacity for multiple
personality, then, is vital to the shamanistic role.

Whatever their nature, it was during her "hidden" years that
HPB (as Theosophists like to call Helena Petrovna Blavatsky)
brought her shamanistic capacities to full flower. Independent
documentation for these wandering years is scant and ambiguous.
It is clear, though, that HPB surfaced in Cairo in 1871, where she
founded a short-lived Spiritualist group. After a brief visit to
Russia, she went to Paris and there was in touch with leading
Spiritualists. Then she came to America.

More significant to us is what must have happened to her inwardly during this time. Whatever she was doing, she was living a
life of marginality to the established social order—all accounts,
flattering and otherwise, agree on this—and was apparently participating more and more actively in another order. In this other order,
the universe itself becomes subjectivity; it is a cosmic mind animated by other subjectivities, later called the Masters and the
Hierarchy. She was half of this world and half of what Theosophists
later called the "inner plane" and the "inner government of the
world," a network or ascendancy or hidden Masters continuous
with intrapsychic forces and directly accessible to consciousness
more than to sense. The frontiers of this realm are probed by
Spiritualism, but, according to Theosophy, though one may be
brought toward it by that faith, its entities are only wretched lorelei
compared to the true splendors of the Masters' occult world.

One could say that the syncretism of Theosophical doctrine, thickly populated with hidden Masters and the lore of many ancient cultures, is an expression on the theoretical level of communitas. It expresses a desire to be free of conditioned structure and to have rapport—an I-thou relationship, one might say—with initiates of all times, places, and levels of reality. The nineteenth-century's romantic bent, inspired by the sensational decoding of the Rosetta Stone, the discovery of the jungle-buried temples of the Mayans and of Angkor, and the unearthing of Troy, was fascinated by lost cities, peoples, even continents. That fascination was fed by books like John L. Stephens's popular *Incidents of Travel in Yucatan,* which as we shall see, Olcott was reading one memorable evening. Of course, the esoteric reputations of Egypt and India go back at least to the days of Plato. Helena Blavatsky and her followers combined old and new by talking of the Brotherhood of Luxor, the Eastern Lodge, the lore of the Mayans, Tibet, Atlantis. A more innocent day than ours is recalled by the syncretistic brooch HPB liked to wear, now preserved in the seal of the Theosophical Society, containing both the swastika and the Star of David, surrounded by the encircling serpent.

Henry Steel Olcott

Colonel Henry Steel Olcott (1832–1907) came later to alienation from the ordinary than did Madame Blavatsky, but no less decisively. He was an energetic, gregarious man who had made a place for himself in the world of practical affairs. He wrote books on agriculture. As a Union officer in the Civil War he was involved in investigative work; his exposure of corrupt suppliers won him recognition. He also had a role in the controversial conspiracy investigation after the assassination of Lincoln. Olcott handled the initial interrogation of Mary Surratt; whether she was a knowing accomplice of John Booth, or her hanging a judicial murder spurred by the overheated atmosphere of Washington in 1865, is still argued. Olcott's material, though, was not formally used in her trial. After the war, Olcott established a reasonably successful law career in New York; he also wrote frequently for newspapers and magazines.

It may be that his separation from his devoutly church-going wife in the early seventies helped induce his break with a conventional life. Perhaps it was nostalgia for the Spiritualism which had during his youth held a fascination for him; around 1850 he spent some time on his uncle's farm in Ohio, and with him had seen some of the early manifestations. As a youth, he had also, like the young Andrew Jackson Davis, experimented with Mesmerism, and once put a girl into a trance for a dental operation. Or perhaps he turned to spirits and theosophy because deep-seated dissatisfaction gnawed at him—though outwardly Olcott seemed a skeptical and sophisticated man about town, more given to a witticism or a convivial drink than to philosophy or prayer.

In any case, as we have seen, his interest in the spirit world was revived in 1874 by reports of the materializations being produced at the home of the dour Eddy Brothers in Vermont. Going to the lonely, ghost-infested New England farm with the intent of writing about it for the *Daily Graphic,* Olcott found himself intrigued by the exotic Russian lady in the red shirt, and the equally exotic apparitions in her train. Before long, back in the city, he had moved into an apartment just above hers, and they were spending all their free time together, talking about Spiritualism and the steps beyond it, experiencing psychic phenomena, and arranging meetings in which these things were made available to a wider circle.

A Remarkable Year

The result of these talks and meetings was the formation of the Theosophical Society in the fall of 1875. Much else, however, happened in that year. Theosophy's precursor was a Miracle Club Olcott organized early in 1875 to investigate psychic phenomena; it was inspired by a group of the same name founded in London around Bulwer-Lytton for the study of magic twenty years before. Olcott's club, however, failed, largely because the medium they selected as the chief object of study turned out to be an utter scoundrel.

In the meantime, HPB continued writing for and corresponding with Spiritualist periodicals, married an unstable Russian and lived briefly with him in Philadelphia, and while in that city passed through a psycho-physical crisis which initiated a remarkable new stage in her spiritual life.

Her correspondence with Spiritualist periodicals involved complicated issues concerning allegedly fraudulent mediumship, and, above all, the attempt of Olcott and Blavatsky to use the magazine called *The Spiritual Scientist* as a vehicle for the teaching said to be coming through them from the "Brotherhood of Luxor," to which HPB belonged. The venture was unsuccessful and ended in bad feelings toward the editor, who later went bankrupt. The failure of this attempt to employ the established means of Spiritualist communication undoubtedly was a factor leading to the founding of the Theosophical Society.

Blavatsky married a Mr. Betanelly, from Russian Georgia, who had entered into correspondence with Olcott and Blavatsky after reading of the Caucasian manifestations at Chittenden. He claimed to be able to verify the identity of one of them. It is conceivable, though totally unproven, that Betanelly knew something, about Chittenden or something else, that HPB desperately wanted unrevealed, even at the cost of a distasteful marital union. HPB agreed to marry her countryman after Betanelly allegedly threatened suicide several times and consented to allow her to keep her name and full freedom. This union ended in divorce in 1878. It was actually never valid, for although HPB apparently chose to assume General Blavatsky was deceased, her aged spouse was, in fact, still alive in the homeland.

Early in 1875 Madame Blavatsky injured her leg twice, once from a fall and once when a bedstead she was trying to move dropped on it. After her move to Philadelphia in March, the leg became gangrene and her condition was very serious. Doctors advised amputation, but this she refused. During June the illness reached a mysterious crisis when, according to Betanelly, during the day she would lie in bed for long hours, immobile and in a deep trance, but at night would get up and proceed to her "spirit room," walking strongly on the diseased limb. She herself wrote on June 19 that she was "tired of all this dying business" and wished she could die once and for all.

Yet she did not die, but during this crisis, according to her own account, went through a remarkable change. Here it is in her own words, from a letter to her sister Mme Jelihovsky in Russia:

> And just about this time [after a sudden cure at the end of June which she attributed to the Master she called the "Sahib"; Olcott says "she got better in one night, by one of her quasi-miraculous cures"] I have

begun to feel a very strange duality. Several times a day I feel that beside me there is someone else, quite separable from me, present in my
body. I never lose the consciousness of my personality; what I feel is
as if I were keeping silent and the one—the lodger who is in me—were
speaking with my tongue.

For instance, I know that I have never been in the places which are
described by my "other me," but this other one—the second me—does
not lie when he tells about places and things unknown to me, because
he has actually seen them and known them well. I have given it up;
let my fate conduct me at its own sweet will; and besides, what am I
to do? It would be perfectly ridiculous if I were to deny the possession
of knowledge avowed by my No. 2, giving occasion to the people
around me to imagine that I kept them in the dark for modesty's sake.

In the night, when I am alone in my bed, the whole life of my No. 2
passes before my eyes, and I do not see myself at all, but quite a different person—different in race and different in feelings. But what's
the use of talking about it? It is enough to drive one mad. I try to throw
myself into the part, and to forget the strangeness of my situation. This
is no mediumship, and by no means an impure power; for that, it has
too strong an ascendancy over us all leading us into better ways. No
devil would act like that. "Spirits," maybe? But if it comes to that, my
ancient "spooks" dare not approach me any more. It's enough for me
to enter the room where a seance is being held, to stop all kinds of
phenomena at once, especially materializations. Ah no, this is alto-
gether of a higher order![3]

HPB referred to this second personality as "the Voice" or "Sahib," and later as her "Master." Apparently this was in time
understood by her to be the same personality as, or sent by, the
the Hindu Master whom she had seen "in the Astral body" as
a child, when he was a sort of guardian angel protecting her
in moments of great danger, and whom she had met in London
in 1851 when he was with the Indo-Nepali delegation and spoke
to her.

The near-death and transformation experience invites comparison with that of Jemima Wilkinson, the Public Universal Friend,
although HPB is characteristically more articulate about it. Regarding its psychological meaning, the light it may shed on her accounts
of remarkable travels and initiation during her hidden years, and its
meaning for her subsequent vocation, the reader must draw his own
conclusions. The summer of 1875 may be the clue to everything,
and one seeking to rationalize in some way the enigma which was

HPB is tempted to seize upon it—but then again, other clues suggest it may seem more important than it really was. The whole scenario may have been partly a working of her "maya." It was neither the first nor last time she underwent such a crisis, or reported diverse personalities working through her. The life of HPB is, in the words of the title of one biography of her, a "hall of magic mirrors."

Nonetheless, there is a strong and deep initiatory motif to the literature of the crisis. During it, Olcott received letters in New York and Boston signed by the Master Serapis, one of his mystic mentors, interpreting the illness as Sister Helena's great initiatory ordeal, when she must fight the dark Dweller on the Threshold (a term from Bulwer-Lytton's novel *Zanoni,* which has much influenced Theosophists and occultists), and "either conquer—or die herself his victim." Olcott hardly mentions the Serapis letters in *Old Diary Leaves*—he is very reticent about the whole affair—but they were published by a later president of the Theosophical Society, C. Jinarajadasa. These epistles interpret not only the illness but also the odd marriage to Betanelly as parts of the initiatory abasement she must pass through. The letters urge Olcott to remain wholly supportive of HPB in her suffering and critical transition; he is told his own initiation depends upon his loyalty to her.[4]

By autumn Olcott and Blavatsky were back together again in New York, the separation and Philadelphia interlude seemingly forgotten. It was then that the Theosophical Society was organized, with full slate of officers and constitution, by a group which had first come together to hear Egyptology lectures by J. H. Felt, and wished to further their pursuit of occult and arcane matters. Colonel Olcott was the first president; H. P. Blavatsky was corresponding secretary. HPB never held any position in the Theosophical Society other than this, except when later she headed the Esoteric Section. Although she was certainly a catalyst in its organization, it would be incorrect to say the society was founded to focus solely on her or on her particular teachings. She undoubtedly would not have been capable of holding an office other than the secretarial one, for public speaking and conducting meetings were tasks she detested and usually refused, and she was quite lacking in either tact or administrative ability.

The Early Years of Theosophy

The infant Theosophical Society in the three years before the journey to India was marked by the erratic shifts in emphasis and membership, yet was lively enough to produce some memorable events. Olcott, in his memoirs *Old Diary Leaves*, reminisces of such things as the alleged first cremation in America, which was held under Theosophical auspices. The deceased was the Baron de Palm, an aristocratic confidence man from Europe who had attached himself to the Theosophists—much to their discomfiture, when the vast wealth and Alpine castles he had promised to leave the society turned out to consist of nothing but a few grubby suitcases followed by a horde of creditors. Olcott also tells of hilarious games of charades played in Madame Blavatsky's apartment, in which Theosophy was spoofed most of all.

But these years were not, however, simply years of chaos. In them occurred a socio-psychological process of great interest, namely, the increasing detachment of the principle Theosophists, Blavatsky and Olcott, from the structures of society at large, as institutional and subjective Theosophy became reified as an alternative reality. There also occurred an event of far-reaching significance, the writing and publication of Madame Blavatsky's first major work, the massive *Isis Unveiled*. Both of these matters influenced the decision to go to India, heartland of the alternative reality probed by the book. These were years of an increasing experience of liminality through the Theosophical mystique, which cried out to be expressed by excursus and to become total, a drive consummated when Olcott knelt on the Bombay docks. But it occurred in different ways for different Theosophists.

For HPB, Theosophy was the culminating phase of a marginal way of life she had lived virtually from birth, in an inward sense. In fact, the responsibilities for leadership she assumed with her position in the society represented a greater accommodation with structure than had ever been forced upon her before, and often she found that accommodation no easy burden to bear, given her anarchic temperament and her relations to the Masters on the other side of mundane structure.

For Olcott, Theosophy and his closeness to Madame Blavatsky were vehicles of transition from a conventionally structured life toward an existence of liminal meaning. When he finally completed the transition with the landing in India he said, doubtless with much relief, that the past was now forgotten. (Later, though, he gravitated toward elaborate structural responsibilities within Theosophy.)

In 1875–78, his marriage was over, but Olcott kept up his professional life with diminishing interest. He symbolized his intrapsychic break through his gleeful participation in such unconventional acts as the cremation and the "Pagan funeral" (as the press called it), mounted for De Palm's obsequies. The last was complete with Orphic and Vedantic hymns and a police cordon to restrain outraged religionists of more orthodox persuasion.

Pulling Olcott toward his new life was his continual exposure to Blavatsky's "phenomena," including letters, signs, and visions from the superhuman Masters of the Brotherhoods of Luxor and the East who were undertaking to teach and guide this willing novice of the Mysteries, this middle-aged attorney who was, in Shelley's phrase, a "nurseling of immortality."

Gertrude M. Williams, in her book on the life of Madame Blavatsky, argues that there was in this period a deliberate and successful attempt by HPB, through psychological pressure reinforced by tricks and magisterial epistles, to wean Olcott away from his past and to get him entirely under her psychic domination.[5] More to the point for the phenomenologist, as we have seen, would be comparison with a complex phenomenon like shamanism.

For the more occasional Theosophist in the New York of the 1870s, Theosophy was a sometime experience of listening to the mysterious lady, colorful, exotic, defiant of convention, talk of arcane marvels and truths far beyond the ken of the ordinary. Within her garishly decorated, book-filled apartment at 46 Irving Place, the lady with the enchanting accent, who suggested remote worlds of monarchical splendor and Eastern mysteries, ushered many into another realm from that of the drab city streets below. Olcott writes:

> Without a single exception those who published accounts of their visits to 'The Lamasery'—as we humorously called our humble suite of rooms—declared that their experience had been novel and out of the usual course. Most of them wrote about HPB in terms of exaggerated praise or wonder. In appearance there was not a shade of the ascetic

about her: she neither mediated in seclusion, practised austerities in regimen, nor selected her company. Her door was open to all, even to those whom she knew meant to write about her with pens over which she could have no control. Often they lampooned her, but if the articles were witty, she used to enjoy them with me to the fullest extent.[6]

What sort of people were involved in early Theosophy? Early members included such luminaries as Thomas A. Edison and General Abner Doubleday, alleged to be the inventor of baseball. A glance at some of the other individuals who appear most prominently in the literature, while not a quantitative survey, does result in some interesting observations, for these persons tend to be, in a technical sense, "marginal" or "status inconsistent." These types, commonly inhabitants past and present of Balch and Nelson's "cultic milieu," are basically people who find that the structures of society do not allow them to be what they experience themselves inwardly to be, or who are forced into a life of several roles which seem inconsistent. They may be people of high intelligence and creativity but with limited formal education and a corresponding lack of access to the regular ways of expression; or they may be people like HPB from the most aristocratic ranks of society, unable to abide its restrictions; or people like immigrants, minorities, the young, the intelligent Victorian (or modern) woman, who, despite some apparent advantages, are never quite sure where they stand, what invisible doors might be closed, and how what they are fits with how they are perceived. In the terms of chapter 3, their social and non-social identities are experienced as highly dissonant. (Maybe even the poorly educated, but brilliant, successful, and spiritually questing Edison was in this category.)

People who experience marginality or status inconsistency often tend to believe their lives are subject to forces outside their control which easily become personified in supernatural forms. They are drawn to associate with groups perceived as reifying their marginality, which can be elevated into the transcendentally liminal, and they may be susceptible to belief (on many levels of terminology and sophistication) in magic and supernatural intervention. (For equally understandable reasons, persons structurally secure and status consistent are prone to establishment religion and the rejection of non-rational interpretations of things.)

HPB perceived something of this, at least in regard to Spiritualism, when she wrote before the beginning of formal Theosophy
that, "not unlike Christianity in the beginning of its era, Spiritualism numbers in its ranks more of the humble and afflicted ones,
than of the powerful and wealthy of this earth."[7] Within the ranks
of the active early Theosophists were rising immigrants like William
Q. Judge and his brother, and H. D. Monachesi. Olcott tells us of a
housepainter extremely well-read in Greek philosophy who became
a member. The Russian Countess de Pashkov, world traveler and
writer, lived for a time with HPB and helped with the cooking.
Charles Sotheran was a bibliophile of independent means. Alexander Wilder, archetype of the profound auto-didact, was a mostly
self-educated practitioner of eclectic medicine, editor, and writer
on esoteric topics.

The Writing of Isis Unveiled

The most significant labor of this period, and the work suggestive
of the process leading to the journey to India, is *Isis Unveiled*
(1877). Started in 1875 or 1876 (inconsistent dates are given), the
writing was apparently a continuation of the same process inaugurated by HPB's strange illness of the summer of 1875, as well as a
work of the budding society. Wilder, Sotheran, the Judge brothers,
and Olcott were involved with the process extensively: they made
suggestions, located sources, transcribed the manuscript for the
publisher, and did indexing. The flow of material came from the
Russian lady, reportedly under inspiration of various of the Masters
who successively inspired the "shell" of her body. As Olcott describes it:

> Now it was a curious fact that each change in the HPB manuscript
> would be preceded, either by her leaving the room for a moment or
> two, or by her going off into the trance or abstracted state, when her
> lifeless eyes would be looking beyond me into space, as it were, and
> returning to the normal waking state almost immediately. And there
> would also be a distinct change of personality, or rather personal pe-
> culiarities, in gait, vocal expression, vivacity of manner, and, above
> all, in temper . . . Not another as to visible change of physical body,
> but another as to tricks of motion, speech, and manners; with different
> mental brightness, different views of things, different command of

English orthography, idiom, and grammar, and different—very, *very*
different command over her temper; which, at its sunniest, was almost
angelic, at its worst, the opposite.[8]

Sometimes it was sufficient that her mentors simply present the
material to her by occult means:

To watch her at work was a rare and never-to-be-forgotten experience.
We sat at opposite sides of one big table usually, and I could see her
every movement. Her pen would be flying over the page, when she
would suddenly stop, look out into space with the vacant eye of the
clairvoyant seer, shorten her vision as though to look at something held
invisible in the air before her, and begin copying on her paper what she
saw. The quotation finished, her eyes would resume their natural expression, and she would go on writing until again stopped by a similar
interruption. I remember well two instances when I, also, was able to
see and even handle books from whose astral duplicates she had copied
quotations into her manuscript, and which she was obliged to "ma-
terialise" for me, to refer to when reading the proofs, as I refused to
pass the pages for the "strike-off" unless my doubts as to the accuracy
of her copy were satisfactory.[9]

Who were these adepts whose invisible fingers were the true
holders of the pen that wrote *Isis Unveiled?* While Theosophy has
no formal or obligatory belief regarding them, it cannot be denied
they were the most intriguing and distinctive idea, or experience,
shared by the intimates of Madame Blavatsky. The concept of the
adepts, later called Masters, however, is far from novel. In this case
it was partly related to Spiritualist belief in spirit guides, but even
more to the primordial *rishis* of Hinduism, the Buddhist bodhisattva, and the psychopomps of theurgic Neoplatonism. Roman
Catholic, Eastern Orthodox, and Muslim saints, especially in popular legend and piety, are entities of about the same order. The
concept is none other than an eclectic revival of the very widespread
belief in human beings who have through great preparation attained participation in a transcendent level of being, like that of the
divine, and so can wield miraculous-seeming wisdom and power.
According to Theosophical tradition, there are beings like this in
many parts of the world and in many faiths; they can communicate
and cooperate with each other, and influence the course of the
world in subtle but significant ways, forming an "invisible government" which does what it can to further humankind's slow evolu-

tion toward the good. India, Tibet, and the Gobi region are their
greatest redoubts. Many Masters are in the physical body, others
work entirely on other planes. But even those in the physical form
can travel or appear out of it through mayavic power; Olcott reports
that some Masters whom they saw appear in New York were later
visited in India, where they manifested nothing other than ordinary
flesh, but were recognizable.

This is the world opened up by *Isis Unveiled*, though that book
actually says little about the Masters. (The rationalization of the
hierarchy of Masters from hints in the writings of HPB and Olcott,
and from further clairvoyant experience, was the work of writers like
C. W. Leadbeater in the second generation of Theosophy.) But the
purpose of the book was not, as the writer acknowledged, to remove
the veil of Isis completely. It was only to lift it a little in order to
suggest the wonders behind the scrim of time and matter. Indeed,
the title was originally intended to be *The Veil of Isis*, and was
changed at the last minute, when it was discovered that another
book of that title existed.

Isis Unveiled is mainly a collage of accounts from the annals of
Mesmerism, history, travel in out-of-the-way places, the lore of
numbers, rites, Masonic symbolism, Pythagoreanism, Neoplatonism, and Hindu and Zoroastrian texts. It is aimed at suggesting an
intricate splendor behind the world as we know it. Significant
concepts of the book are: a supreme mind, pre-existent souls which
have fallen from glory into life on earth, their initiatory purification
and return whence they came, and their acquiring along the path
supernormal powers. These principles are demonstrated by the
anecdotes, which report about events that demonstrate the existence of mind and spiritual realities independent of body and of
birth and death as we know it. The book extols the power of mind
manifested in Mesmerism and magic and brings to light the activity
of disembodied souls and "elementals." The reader of *Isis Unveiled* also joins excursions into speculative history that round off
an alternative world view; compares the traditional lives of Krishna,
the Buddha, and Jesus; and confronts sardonic remarks on "orthodox" Christianity and science alike.

In all of this India appears as a beckoning contrast. It is an
unfailing source of stories of marvels illustrative of the main theses,

many taken from the voluminous and wonder-filled books of L. Jacolliot, or of the Abbè Huc, though some are presented as first hand observations of HPB, or possibly of one of her possessing entities. India, moreover, had not paled under the grip of either church or gown as we know them in the West, but its wise ones rejoiced in a deep philosophy not far fallen from its source in primordial truth. Indeed, though the ruling doctrine of the book is said to be Platonic, *Isis* asserts that the wisdom of the West's profoundest mind is but a compendium of "the abstruse systems of old India" which are thousands of years older.[10]

It is clear, then, that the compiling of *Isis Unveiled* was an important step along the way to India, though not the only one.[11] Let us now trace the steps of that progress.

Going East

It is not entirely clear just when and why the two leading Theosophists determined to depart for India. But it is evident that it turned out to be a remarkably sagacious move. Despite the publication of *Isis Unveiled* in 1877, and the attention it attracted, the Theosophical Society seemed to have reached a dead end in New York. Olcott, in a later, double-funnel chronological diagram of the society's vicissitudes, shows it declining to a mere point at the time of the pilgrimage to India, and then, after the trip, the diagram grows broader and broader with the proliferation of new chapters there and elsewhere.

But in these three years of decline, India, always a major reservoir of the ancient wisdom Theosophy was concerned to revive, came more and more into their conversations. The supernormal Masters whom Madame Blavatsky was able to introduce to Olcott increasingly wore turbans. Then in 1878 the society united by correspondence with Swami Dayananda Sarasvati's Arya Samaj (founded in 1875 to affirm the Vedas as revealed scripture and to reform Hinduism on that basis), calling itself "The Theosophical Society of the Arya Samaj." Olcott, president of the Theosophical Society, felt at the time that the Arya Samaj's reconstructed Vedism was one with the spiritual universalism he identified with Theosophy, and HPB affirmed that Dayananda was none other than a Himalayan Master

inhabiting the great swami's body. But vast was Olcott's disillusionment, confirmed later in India, when further information
revealed the Arya Samaj, for all its virtues, intended only conservative, integralist reforms and the advancement of education in India,
and so was of little interest to Western universalists, unless from a
larger perspective than Olcott could then comprehend.

The relation with the Arya Samaj had its roots in 1870, when
Olcott had met Moolji Thackersey of Bombay on a ship to England.
In 1878 Olcott began corresponding with him again, and invited
the Indian to join the Theosophical Society. Thackersey, in turn,
told Olcott in enthusiastic terms of the allegedly parallel work of
the Arya Samaj, and introduced him by mail to Hurrychund Chintamon, president of the Bombay branch of the Arya Samaj. It
appears that this relationship, unhappy as it turned out to be,
sowed the seeds of the desire to go to India. Olcott and Blavatsky
now had a definite reason for going: to meet Saravati Dayananda,
the great spiritual leader of the Samaj, learn Eastern esotericism
from him, and strengthen the links between the two societies.
Having specific contacts in India also made the practical side of the
trip seem more manageable. Even after the first disillusionment in
New York upon getting further information about the Arya Samaj,
they still felt drawn to Aryavarta, and HPB still felt that Sarasvati
was a great Master who was summoning her. Correspondence was
continued, and a little later Chintamon was entrusted with making
arrangements in India for the arrival of the New York Theosophists
—a trust they were sorely to regret.

Another reason for the journey to India in 1878 was the founding
of a London branch of the society that year, which the two wanted
to visit en route. Moreover, that same year HPB became the first
immigrant Russian woman to acquire U.S. citizenship, making her
eligible for an American passport. The change of citizenship was
emotionally difficult for her. It was inconsistent with other posi-
tions of hers, HPB admitted, but she retained to the end a deep
love for Russia, the Czar, and the Orthodox Church—which never
shared in the scathing attacks she heaped on the priestcraft of Rome
and the fanaticism of Protestants, and whose last rites she is said to
have requested quietly at the end of her occult mission.[12] But the
British Raj's almost-paranoid suspicions of Russian designs on India

at the time made it far more politic for this unusual traveler to carry a U.S. than a Russian passport—even though it did not relieve her of a discreet police "tail" during some of her stay in the land of elephants and sages, and even though her adversaries often accused her, among other things, of being a spy.

Still another reason for going to India was that the famous levitationist and "physical medium" D. D. Home, whose pupil and assistant some report HPB to have once been (though she denied it bitterly), and who was well-connected in Russia, published a book called *Lights and Shadows of Spiritualism* in 1877. It included a chapter ridiculing the Theosophical Society and reviling Olcott as a fool. HPB was furious. On October 2, 1877, she wrote the Russian psychical researcher A. N. Aksakov, "That's why I'm going off forever to India, and from shame and grief I wish to go where no one knows even my name. Home has ruined me forever in Europe by his spite and hatred."[13]

The decision had also a powerful occult side. As we have seen, India had been a part of HPB's subjective world at least since she was twenty, when she had met her lord on the inner plane in London, probably he who later became known as the Rajput prince Morya. "By the light of the moon that was setting," she had seen "the Master of my dreams!!" she wrote later in her diary with schoolgirlish rapture of meeting him at Ramsgate (probably a disguise for London) on her twentieth birthday, and she had sought the princely great soul around the world ever since.[14]

It was said to be the Masters, including some from India, who actually ordered the Theosophists to leave America for India in 1878, just as HPB had said it was under orders that she had come to America five years before. Following are some intriguing lines from her diary late in 1878; Gertrude Williams suspected them of having been written after the move to India and backdated, but in any case they offer a Theosophical hermeneutic of the journey.[15]

In the diary for October 22, 1878 (they left December 17 of the same year), we read, "*Narayan* left watch—and in came *Sahib*. The latter with orders from Serapis to complete all the first days of December."[16] In this enigmatic passage, Narayan is an Indian Master, later identified with an actual living swami in the hills not far from Madras, whom HPB and Olcott met physically about April

30, 1882, and who supported the Theosophists in a time of trouble. Sahib, whom we have already encountered, probably refers to Morya. Serapis was prominent in the early days of Theosophy when Olcott was still studying with the Egyptian section, and signed the letters he received during HPB's psycho-physiological crisis. The curious change of watch among these Masters suggests the subjective "overshadowing" by these supernormal entities which was involved in the writing of *Isis Unveiled* and was apparently a major component of HPB's inner experience.

Later, on November 14, we have these lines: "Naray decamped and Morya walked in—broken finger and all. Came with definite orders from Serapis. *Have to go;* the latest from 15th to 20th Dec.... O God, O Indra of the golden face! Is this really the beginning and the end!"[17]

Of a somewhat earlier period, Olcott tells us:

> Little by little, HPB let me know of the existence of Eastern adepts, and their powers, and gave me by a multitude of phenomena the proofs of her own control over the occult forces of nature.... For years, and until shortly before I left New York for India, I was connected in pupilage with the African section of the Occult Brotherhood; but, later, when a certain wonderful psycho-physiological change happened to HPB that I am not at liberty to speak about, and that nobody has up to the present suspected, although enjoying her intimacy and full confidence, as they fancy, I was transferred to the Indian section and a different group of Masters.[18]

Even more revealing is the following account by Olcott, unfortunately not dated, but presumably in 1876 or 1877, since they were at work on *Isis Unveiled;* for Olcott, this event was apparently the decisive supernatural goad in the direction of India.

> The story has been told before, but it had its place in the present retrospect, for it was the chief among the causes of my abandonment of the world and my coming out to my Indian home. Hence it was one of the chief factors in the upbuilding of the Theosophical Society. I do not mean to say that without it I should not have come to India, for my heart had been leaping within me to come, from the time when I learned what India had been to the world, what she might be made again. An insatiable longing had possessed me to come to the land of the Rishis and the Buddhas, the Sacred Land among lands; but I could not see my way clear to breaking the ties of circumstance which bound me to America, and I might have felt compelled to put

it off to that "convenient season" which so often never comes to the procrastinator and waiter upon the turn of events. This experience in question, however, settled my fate; in an instant doubts melted away, the clear foresight of a fixed will showed the way, and before the dawn of that sleepless night came, I began to devise the means and to bend all things to that end. The happening was thus:

Our evening's work on *Isis* was finished, I had bade good-night to HPB, retired to my own room, closed the door as usual, sat me down to read and smoke, and was soon absorbed in my book; which, if I remember aright, was Stephens's *Travels in Yucatan;* at all events, not a book on ghosts . . .

All at once, as I read with my shoulder a little turned from the door, there came a gleam of something white in the right-hand corner of my right eye; I turned my head, dropped my book in astonishment, and saw towering above me in his great stature an Oriental clad in white garments, and wearing a head-cloth or turban of amber-striped fabric . . . [19]

Olcott continues at great length to tell us of the splendor, the majesty, and the spiritual radiance of this man, which caused him to bend his knees and bow as before a god. But the mighty presence bade the colonel be seated, and, sitting down himself, proceeded to tell Olcott about the great work for humanity which lay before him and about the mysterious tie that had drawn the colonel and HPB together. Finally he left, and as he did so he placed his turban (which can still be seen at the Theosophical headquarters in Adyar) on the table as a tangible proof of his appearance. Olcott then immediately banged on HPB's door to tell her of this marvelous experience.

India was, first of all, the land of phenomenal Masters, who could reach out to touch the thoughts and even appear before the eyes of one half a world away, and whose presence made their native home a magnet. They practiced "Brahma Vidya" or "Eastern Spiritualism," and it was the power of these Masters who summoned the Westerners, for their "invisible government of the world" had conceived a plan for the advancement of the world in which they would be its roving ambassadors. The pilgrimage to India was part voyage of discovery, part response to a call from what Victor Turner calls "the center out there," the goal of all pilgrimage. The journey took on the traditional structure of a pilgrimage, and was consummated like all such in a situation of full liminality and communitas.

Passage to More Than India

Beyond all other reasons for the journey, then, was the unparalleled
spiritual magnetism of India and enigmatic Tibet. The journey
itself was long and difficult. They left the United States on December 17, 1878, and, after a stop-over in England, arrived in India in
mid-February of the following year. The meaning India had come
to have for them—and for many other occidental seekers—is finely
expressed by Olcott in his *Old Diary Leaves*. He writes that upon
finally landing in Bombay on February 16, 1879:

> the first thing I did on touching land was to stoop down and kiss the
> granite step; my instinctive act of pooja! For here we were at last on
> sacred soil; our past forgotten, our perilous and disagreeable sea-voyage
> gone out of mind, the agony of long deferred hopes replaced by the
> thrilling joy of presence in the land of the Rishis, the cradle country
> of religions, the dwelling place of the Masters, the home of our dusky
> brothers and sisters, with whom to live and die was all we could desire.[20]

In these lines is certainly expressed the sacred and archetypal
meaning of pilgrimage, and understanding the inner meaning of
pilgrimage is a valuable key to understanding the meaning of
Theosophy, with its restlessness toward the conventional and its
quest for occult lore and initiations, for the source and inner
meaning of religions, and for human brotherhood.

In the passage to India Olcott, through peril and strain, found
movement away from the ordinary through a ritually demarcated
threshold, to a place at once inductive of a new sort of awareness
("the thrilling joy of presence in the land of the Rishis"), a return
to a point of origins ("the cradle country of religions"), a region of
access to transcendence ("the dwelling place of the Masters"), and
the locale of a new, transvalued community ("the home of our
dusky brothers and sisters") establishing ultimate communitas
rather than conditioned relationships ("with whom to live and die
was all we could desire").

Much the same symbolic experience, as Victor Turner has shown,
can be found in established ritual pilgrimage: the medieval journey
to Jerusalem, the Muslim *hajj*, Hindu progresses to Hardwar or
Pandharpur.[21] But the Theosophical Twins were travelling no well-
worn sacred track, nor was it one particular shrine or peak that drew

them, except the presence of Swami Dayananda. Olcott, at least, may hardly have known India well enough to single out such places. Rather it was India itself, one might say the idea of India, and its invisible realities, which was the object of pilgrimage.

Gustave Moreau's overwhelming late-romantic painting ''The Triumph of Alexander,'' catches something of this sort of vision of the East: the Macedonian hero rides before a topless mountain laden with Egyptian columns, Hindu temples, a Jaina tirthankara, a Buddha from the Ajanta caves, all bathed in the opalescent light of the enchanted Orient. The same undifferentiated but romantically mystical East earlier appeared in the writings of Henry David Thoreau, whose importance for the emergent and excursus tradition in America should not be underestimated, and who mused of it:

> While the commentators are disputing about the meaning of this word and that, I hear only the resounding of the ancient sea, and put into it all the meaning I am possessed of, the deepest murmurs I can recall, for I do not in the least care where I get my ideas, or what suggests them.[22]

In counterbalance to this mood, however, it should be pointed out that Thoreau, probably more than Emerson, was quite aware of the diverse cultures and major spiritual texts of the East, and could cite them with some precision. A combination of textual specificity and the romantic vision of the East is found in this famous passage from *Walden,* which gloriously evokes the universalism, the antihistoricism, the mystical intuitionism, and the romance of the ''Yankee Hindoo,'' despite several factual improbabilities.

> In the morning I bathe my intellect in the stupendous and cosmogonal philosophy of the Bhagvat-Geeta, since whose composition years of the gods have elapsed, and in comparison with which our modern world and its literature seem puny and trivial; and I doubt if that philosophy is not to be referred to a previous state of existence, so remote is its sublimity from our conceptions. I lay down the book and go to my well for water, and lo! there I meet the servant of the Bramin, priest of Brahma and Vishnu and Indra, who still sits in his temple on the Ganges reading the Vedas, or dwells at the root of a tree with his crust and water jug. I meet his servant come to draw water for his master, and our buckets at it were grate together in the same well. The pure Walden water is mingled with the sacred water of the Ganges.[23]

Even more suggestive is Walt Whitman's "Passage to India," written in 1871 to commemorate the completion of the transcontinental railroad, the Trans-Atlantic cable, and above all the Suez Canal through which the Theosophical Twins were to pass a few years later on their way to that fabled heartland of the soul. It contains lines such as these:

Passage O soul to India!
Eclaircise the myths Asiatic, the primitive fables.
Not you alone proud truths of the world,
Nor you alone ye facts of modern science,
But myths and fables of old, Asia's, Africa's fables,
The far-darting beams of the spirit, the unloos'd dreams,
The deep diving bibles and legends,
The daring plots of the poets, the elder religions;
O you temples fairer than lilies pour'd over by the rising sun!
O you fables spurning the known, eluding the hold of the known,
   mounting to heaven!
You lofty and dazzling towers, pinnacled, red as roses, burnish'd
   with gold!
Towers of fables immortal fashion'd from mortal dreams!...
Passage to more than India!
Are thy wings plumed indeed for such far flights?
O soul, voyagest thou indeed on voyages like those?
Disportest thou on waters such as those?
Soundest below the Sanscrit and the Vedas?
Then have thy bent unleash'd.
Passage to you, your shores, ye aged fierce enigmas!
... Passage to more than India!
O secret of the earth and sky!

The Western discovery of spiritual India has been for some a passage into an archetypal Far Place which transforms them and incorporates them into a new community. For them, as for Blavatsky and Olcott, passage to India has been a journey to another spiritual state as well as to another land. It has been Hermann Hesse's paradigmatic "Journey to the East"—which has been made by many who have never physically left Europe or America. But for all of them (whatever it may be in itself), India has been the land of communitas relations with others and with spiritual reality, the land of return to sunrise origins, the sacred place which is at once the pivot of the spiritual world and the place of access to transcendence. It has been the true goal of pilgrimage, what Turner calls "the center out there."

In India Olcott and Blavatsky lived with a communitas-like detachment from all ties except those of the quest, and entered more and more deeply into subjective freedom from the structures imposed by their previous lives. Olcott tells us of the wonderful first days in the Asian land:

> Every evening we held an impromptu durbar, when the knottiest problems of philosophy, metaphysics, and science were discussed. We lived and breathed in an atmosphere of mind, amid the highest spiritual ideals . . .
>
> Visitors kept on crowding our bungalow, and stopping until late every evening to discuss religious questions. Old and young, it was all the same; and thus did we come, so early in our connection with the Hindus, to know the difference between Western and Eastern ideals of life, and the greater dignity of the latter. Questions of wealth, color, business, or politics scarcely ever crossed our threshold; the Soul was the burning topic of debate. . . .
>
> Fanatics, if you please; crazy enthusiasts; dreamers of unpractical dreams; devotees of a hobby! dupes of our imaginations. Yet our dreams were of human perfectibility, our yearnings after divine wisdom, our sole hope to help mankind to higher thinking and nobler living. And, under those umbrageous palms, we were visited in person by Mahātmas; and their inspiring presence made us strong to proceed in the path we were treading . . .[23]

One must keep in mind that this was British India in the heyday of imperialism and the Christian, Anglo-Saxon chauvinism which too often went with it, not least among India's fair-skinned rulers, to comprehend fully the radical reversal of established structures implied by Olcott's attitude. They traveled continually—perhaps in itself a symbol of breaking structure. When one thinks of conditions of travel in nineteenth century India, it is tiring even to read Olcott's narrative.

They intrigued the cream of Anglo-Indian society at Simla. Olcott also lectured to native audiences on the virtues of their own heritage and did Mesmeric "magnetic" healings to all who drew near at innumerable stops. Blavatsky mysteriously kept in touch with the Masters, from whom letters arrived frequently during these early Indian years. Far from familiar kin and culture, in defiance of convention in all sorts of ways—from their lack of Christian piety,

to their unimperial attitude toward natives, to their strange un-
married companionship—they had nonetheless found for themselves in India an inner space for communitas between male and
female, between European and Asiatic, between religions, between
this world and a transcendent one represented by the Masters.

Their life in India was an acting-out of the different perspective
on the human scene cast by the Theosophical teaching that Masters
of the Ancient Wisdom stood behind all religions, a teaching
reinforced by the phenomena associated with Madame Blavatsky
from the obscure farm at Chittenden to the bungalow in Bombay.
During the nineteenth century, despite the Transcendentalists and
their kin, most people thought of culture, above all spiritual culture, as flowing only from West to East in the form of missionaries,
traders, and imperial proconsuls. As quaint as the mission of the
Theosophical Twins may sound to some, it was a destiny-fraught
sign of a rising undertow to that flow, a reverse process which would
not stop until independence had come again to the East and the
West was awash with yoga and chanting. In the Indian subcon-
tinent that mission had an important part in the recovery of pride
in indigenous culture at the roots of the independence movement.
Olcott is something of a national hero in Sri Lanka (Ceylon) for his
work for the revitalization of Buddhism and was recently honored
there on a postage stamp. In the West, Theosophy, though never
large numerically or politically important, has had through books
and lectures a certain role in popularizing such concepts as karma
and reincarnation, and in promoting a view of spiritual traditions
neither reductionistic nor incompatible with tolerance.

India as "Center Out There"

Let us reconsider some of the reasons why Olcott and Blavatsky
went to India. As pilgrimage to a place of wider liminality, it was
because early Theosophy did not find a secure place structurally in
New York—that is, the organization did not appear then to have a
promising future—but at the same time it had opened up for the
core-group a subjective world too big to be contained in the Irving
Place apartment. There was a need for movement in space to equal
the increasing expansion of mind. Having become a liminal person

inwardly, Olcott in particular needed a place where he could in-
tegrate himself by acting out the liminal role in a totally new life; it
would have been less meaningful for him to kiss the pavement in
New York!

In India, Blavatsky and Olcott could act out liminality and the
"exaltation of the weak" motif so closely related to it which we
discussed in connection with Spiritualism. They were outsiders in
that rigidly structured society, religious "bums" who attracted
attention at all levels. True, Olcott and HPB were not structurally
weak by circumstance but by choice, like many "dropouts" of our
day. But they had made their decision, and, indeed, had little
future in the West. In India, though, it was another game; whether
they had anticipated it or not, Theosophy became a sensation there,
and the Theosophical Twins found themselves the guests and the
subject of gossip of common people, maharajahs, pandits, and the
British elite. By an odd coincidence, the Viceroy of India at the
time of their arrival was the romantic imperialist Robert Bulwer-
Lytton, son of Edward George Bulwer-Lytton, whose occult novels
like *Zanoni* had so much affected HPB and other Theosophists. His
presence in India made talk of such matters fashionable in the
drawing-rooms of Simla and "Ooty."

For the Theosophists themselves, India was "the center out
there" which incarnated their vision. As represented in such
accounts as those of Jacolliot, it was a land of marvels like those of
antiquity in the days of the "Ancient Mystery Schools" had been.
Excursus religion as means of access to liminality in American
society needs continually to refresh its ties to the reservoirs of liminal
infinity to which it relates. For this reason pilgrimage is frequently
of more importance to emergent than to established religion. Theosophists go to India, and American adherents of Nichiren Shoshu
or Zen to Japan, proportionately much more than American Meth-
odists go to Jerusalem or even Aldersgate. On a deeper level, one
feels the subjective freedom from ordinary structure of the excursus
religionist needs to be symbolized and sustained by frequent com-
ings and goings; for this reason leaders, like Blavatsky and Olcott,
are virtually peripatetic.

Finally, communitas, as the goal to which liminality inexorably
pressed Olcott and HPB, required a social setting which nine-

teenth-century India admirably provided. They could only find it
in a society in which they were wholly marginal, yet in which they
would have effective access to many different levels. English-speak-
ing and cultivated, but non-British and non-Hindu (in traditional
terms), India was open to them as it would not have been to one
who had a place high or low in its complex and rigid structure; they
could fall into the interstices of social structure while amusing or
enlightening people of all sorts, and could exercise the ability of the
"status inconsistent" to rejoice in those miracles and alternative
world views which the establishmentarian fears.

In both practical and psychic terms, then, India represented an
ideal "center out there," peripheral to European-American society,
yet accessible in terms of language and steamship bookings; full of
Masters of Wisdom yet, under the British Raj, just familiar enough
that one could meaningfully be marginal to it.

Nor can one overlook the subjective history of Olcott and HPB in
1875–78, however one explains it. Out of it came the determina-
tion to go to India. Something suggested by the transfer of Olcott
from the African to the Indian sections of the Occult Brotherhood,
by his midnight turbaned visitor, by HPB's mysterious crisis and
the insistent orders from Serapis, underscored the logic of the outer
events.

It was in India that the marvelous happened continuously to
the Theosophists, even to a Master awakening Olcott in the middle
of the night in a tent near Lahore to hand him a silk-wrapped letter,
and the celebrated and controversial "astral post office" of the
"shrine room" at Adyar where such communication appeared
regularly. To be sure, much of the literature of early Theosophy
now has a quintessential Victorian flavor, charming but distancing.
Yet the magic that India was to them, as old as Apollonius of Tyana
and as new as the most recent American guru-enthusiasm, is with
us still. It is paradigmatically exemplified in the pilgrimages of
Olcott and Blavatsky and their followers. They were sometimes
credulous, undoubtedly, but they anticipated in important ways
the more pluralistic, culturally interdependent, and subjectivity-
oriented spiritual world of the twentieth century in which India
remains an unequaled symbol of the spiritual side of all those
things. One could almost say India, or perhaps the East, is to

excursus religion since the Theosophical transformation of Spiritualism what Palestine is to the American religious establishment.

Notes on the Destiny of Theosophy

Theosophy, then, provided a wedge for liminality to the nineteenth and twentieth centuries—and to what lies beyond liminality. Our purpose here has been just to focus on one "moment" in the actualization of liminality, the journey to India of 1878–79. But what was started then was to continue. The complex history of Theosophy, fascinating as it is, cannot be fully traced here. However, the movements devolving from Theosophy might be cited as illustrating ways in which a Theosophy-based experience of liminality can change and grow.

Alice Bailey (1880–1949), founder of the Arcane School and the Full Moon Meditation Groups, and Guy Ballard (1878–1939) of the "I Am" movement, are representative of those who have started activites based on new and special communications from Theosophical Masters. Alice Bailey wrote a series of books under inspiration of one called "The Tibetan" which, within the context of Theosophical doctrine, put special emphasis on the imminent coming of the Christ and the importance of meditation by groups, which customarily meet every full moon to create lines of spiritual force preparing for this event. Ballard's "I Am" has stressed contact with "Ascended Masters" and the use of sound and color in the spiritual life; it is also highly eschatological. In both cases the liminality experience inauguraged by talk of Theosophical Masters has led, more than in regular Theosophy, to an almost apocalyptic sense that the ordinary, non-liminal world is about to pass away.

On the other hand, Jiddu Krishnamurti (b. 1895), himself a son of India, "the center out there," was raised by the post-Blavatsky generation of Theosophists as one who was to become the voice of the World Teacher for this age "if he proved worthy"—virtually the one whom the Bailey school anticipates. But in 1929, when he was expected to begin his full mission, he renounced it in any formal sense together with any idea of philosophical or spiritual conceptual knowledge or organization. Since then Krishnamurti has traveled the world, lecturing on behalf of a way of thought free from all cages built by thought-forms, memories, and desires. Over

the years, his books and lectures have become immensely popular.
Here is a formless incarnation of the liminality first broached in the
Theosophical journey to India. Liminality is the freedom and reversal of breaking structure; structure can be broken by the marvelous,
but it can also be broken when the here-and-now is freed from both
the marvelous and the ordinary.[25]

The theosophical journey of the 1870s set in motion the historical
forces which led to both these ends. It established models for the
excursus religion pilgrimage to the East and established the symbolic role of India or Tibet as source of liberating wisdom. Since
then, India has increasingly been either a place where one goes on
the seeker's pilgrimage, or the place from which have come teachers
like Swami Vivekananda and others of the Ramakrishna Mission
and the Vedanta Societies, or Swami Yogananda of the Self-Realization Fellowship, or Swami Bhaktivedanta of the International
Society for Krishna Consciousness, or Guru Maharaj Ji of the Divine
Light Mission. The journey of the Russian lady and the American
gentleman a century ago can help us to understand the inner
meaning of this ongoing exchange.

6   *Zen Journeys to the West*

Krishnamurti and Zen

Is Krishnamurti the true end of Theosophy? Despite conventional Theosophy's elaborate metaphysical doctrines about the evolution of worlds and humanities according to triads and septads and so forth, does the mentalism that underlies it finally agree with Krishnamurti that all our concepts and ideas are empty and a hindrance to the fullness of joy? There is some reason to think so; Krishnamurti's books are popular among Theosophists, and even a Theosophical classic such as Mabel Collins's *Light on the Path,* first published in 1885, ten years before Krishnamurti was born, ends with such enigmatic, concept-transcending verses as

> Hold fast to that which has neither substance nor existence.
> Listen only to the voice which is soundless.
> Look only on that which is invisible alike to the inner and the outer sense.

In the light of a spiritual path as sublimely austere as is suggested by these lines, the ornate side of Theosophical thought would have to be seen as a true yet disposable vision, important only at certain stages of the long ascent to a whiteness without shadow.

These are ideas, or rather anti-ideas, which also suggest the way of Zen Buddhism, especially as it has been presented in the West. For at the heart of Zen are texts like the Heart Sutra and the Diamond Sutra; the former has lines like

> There is no suffering, no accumulation, no annihilation, no path;
> there is no knowledge, no attainment, no realization, because there

is no attainment. In the mind of the bodhisattva who dwells depending
on the wisdom that has gone beyond, there are no obstacles, and going
beyond thought-coverings, he reaches final Nirvana.

Links between Theosophy and Krishnamurti, and the recent
enthusiasms for Zen in America, are perceptible on the historical as
well as the theoretical plane; Alan Watts, who certainly did more
than anyone else except his mentor D. T. Suzuki to popularize Zen
in America in the mid-twentieth century, was introduced to Suzuki
as a young man in London in the 1930s by Christmas Humphreys,
an old-guard Theosophist who established the Buddhist Lodge in
England, and by Krishnamurti. For that matter, the wife of D. T.
Suzuki, the American Beatrice Lane Suzuki, a notable Buddhist
scholar in her own right, was an active Theosophist and organizer of
the work in Japan.[1] Mircea Eliade tells us that Edward Conze, whose
admirable scholarly books on Buddhism have also done much to
spread Buddhist thought in the West, likewise professed Theosophy and was a great admirer of *The Secret Doctrine*. Conze believed, among other things, that Madam Blavatsky was a reincarnation of Tsonkapa, the great Tibetan Buddhist reformer of the four-
teenth century.[2] Historical and personal ties between the Theosophy
of the earlier decades of the century and the Buddhist enthusiasms
of the fifties and sixties are, then, far from lacking. An egregious
symbol of the linkage is the famous mid-fifties "underground"
movie *Pull My Daisy*, which Jack Kerouac, to be discussed in a
moment, narrated and which was based on an earlier play of his; it
consists largely of a conversation between a bishop of the Theo-
sophically oriented Liberal Catholic Church and several leading
"beats."

Theosophy has had a significant general influence on this century. It is sufficient to mention its impact on the images and
spiritual development of William Butler Yeats, and the fact that
Mohandas K. Gandhi first discovered the *Bhagavad-Gita*, which
was to become virtually his Bible, in a Theosophical edition. Indeed, closer to home, the prevalence of ideas like karma, reincarnation, astrology, and a "new age" in popular culture owes a debt to
the lectures and literature-distribution of Theosophists in American
towns and cities as far back as the 1890s. One can find Theosophical
books in public libraries almost everywhere; they have been read,

and have influenced the inner worlds of countless people, including some who are outwardly pillars of more conventional churches. It is worth noting that the immensely popular teachings about reincarnation and Atlantis of the Kentucky seer Edgar Cayce seem to be taken from Theosophical lore. Such recent and very widely read books as those of Ruth Montgomery, Richard Bach's *Jonathan Livingstone Seagull,* and Raymond Moody's *Life after Life,* with its data on postmortum experience, also agree in a Swedenborgian-Spiritualist-Theosophical view of the soul and its career after physical death.

Yet, while the teachings may be timeless, the Theosophical vessel as we know it has an unmistakably nineteenth-century aura about it—part of its glamour to some, suggestive of stuffiness and tedium to others. There is the heavily verbal orientation of the lectures and ponderous books, and the mystical systems seemingly as baroque as the fittings of a Victorian parlor. In America, Theosophy inherited to some extent the place of the Spiritualism of the 1840s and 50s. So has Theosophy in the mid-twentieth century given center stage to other expressions of emergent religion. These have often been imports brought more or less intact from the East, complete with foreign-language terminology and teachers in foreign-looking robes. It would seem than many American seekers have wanted the flavor of an alternative culture as well as the words of an alternative faith, and have preferred the appearance of integralism in the exotic faith to syncretism—the latter having, unjustly, a pejorative connotation.

This is, no doubt, symptomatic of increasing alienation from much of American culture on the part of those who are seekers. They do not desire, as did an earlier generation of aficionados of the East, reassuring symbols of continuity with the past: a service with a basically Protestant structure at 11 on Sunday morning, group organization with American-style boards and committees, and an emphasis on reading scripturelike books and listening to sermonistic lectures as the major means of communication. However Eastern the message, these Western features of worship and sociological packaging, typical of groups like the Vedanta societies and Self-Realization Fellowship, make it seem continuous with liberal Protestantism—even as the message itself is likely to be couched in terms that make it seem an extension of Emerson.

But in the generations after World War II, a new pattern in the expression of emergent and excursus religion appeared. It had a definite religious content, Eastern more often than not, but it sought symbols of discontinuity with the American churchly past, at the same time incorporating not only the ideology but also aspects of the culture and lifestyle of the land of its origin. Americans practicing yoga or Zen, chanting "Hare Krishna" or "Nam myoho renge kyo," had their meetings at any time other than on Sunday morning. Their gatherings to sit silently in lotus posture, or chant in an exotic tongue in an atmosphere of incense and strange gods, would not have been reassuring to even the most liberal of old-fashioned Boston Unitarians. And they would often favor the dress, the food and tea and art, of India or Japan. But, as we shall see, now the wheel has almost come full circle, and in a movement like est, ideas typical of the alternative altars are being programmed in management-seminar format.

Zen Buddhism has no doubt been the most widely influential, at least culturally, of these imports. Paradoxically, Zen has conspicuously played the role of exotic import, and yet has been the most readily assimilated of the Eastern imports in America.

Zen Buddhism

A glance at the history and meaning of Zen in Asia is essential if we are to understand why Zen in particular emerged in America as a symbolic focus for emergent and excursus religion.

The word *Zen* is the Japanese transliteration of the Chinese *Ch'an,* which, in turn, is a transliteration of the Sanskrit *dhyana,* meaning meditation. Zen, then, is that tradition of practice which emphasizes meditation as the chief means to realizing Buddhist enlightenment. In a Zen temple in Japan or in an American Zen center, one will see rows of Zen practitioners seated in the posture called *zazen*—legs crossed in the lotus position, back erect, eyes half-open, focused on the floor or a wall some four feet in front, hands in the lap with thumbs joined. As they sit, a proctor with a stick may walk slowly up and down before the silent figures, bringing it down smartly on the shoulder of one who becomes drowsy or who bows forward to indicate he needs its therapy to recall him to mindfulness. A slowly burning stick of incense before the altar measures the calm minutes as they slip by; when the *zazen* session is over, a sharp striking of clappers and gongs will break into the tranquility. When the meditators arise to labor, eat, or solicit alms, they are to do it in a manner demonstrating the true nature of the self approached in *zazen*.

This is concentration of a particular sort. It is not thinking gorgeous thoughts, or contacting spirit worlds, but is "sitting quietly, doing nothing," allowing an "empty but marvelous" consciousness to surface. The things one may do with the mind during *zazen*—counting breaths, following thoughts until they vanish, holding in consciousness one of those enigmatic Zen *koans* or riddles—are all ways of stopping the activity of the "monkey mind." They are ways of bringing to a halt the ordinary racing of the stream of consciousness and the ordinary tendency to interpret experience conceptually and rationally, and to enable one to think spontaneously and to see things "just as they are."

Zen has two sides. There is the still meditation and the harsh discipline, and then there is the spirit of liberation from all constraints. Alan Watts called them square Zen and beat Zen.[3]

These two sides appear throughout the long history of Zen. According to tradition, Zen began long ago when the Buddha handed a flower to a disciple and smiled—and the disciple caught in the flower and smile a universe of wisdom outside all words and books. The secret of that smile was passed on until it was brought by Bodhidharma to China in 520 A.D. Actually, Ch'an is a distinctively Chinese form of Mahayana Buddhism which combines the latter's deep psychology and metaphysics with a Taoist sense of naturalness and nature and a characteristic Chinese pragmatism. It flourished in the great T'ang dynasty (618-907), and eventually came to be the normative Buddhism of most Chinese monasteries. Ch'an was brought by Eisai and Dogen to Japan in the thirteenth century, where—although never more than one of several Buddhist denominations—Zen became popular with the samurai class then ruling the island empire and had a powerful cultural influence.

Throughout its history, Zen has known its share of stern disciplinarians, in whose temples one ate and slept little, where rising and sitting and walking were done with military precision, and where interviews with pupils were not lacking in shouts and blows.

Zen has also produced a small but madcap assortment of hermits, wanderers, and poets. In T'ang China, there was Han Shan, the eccentric Cold Mountain recluse whose poems were translated by Gary Snyder—of this more later. In medieval Japan, Ikkyu, awakened to a desire for enlightenment by hearing the call of a crow in the deep of night, tempered the monastic life with wanderings through the countryside. Though of imperial blood, he mixed with all sorts of people gladly, ate meat, drank sake, and begat children. Yet the Zen teaching of this "son of the errant cloud," as he called himself, was hard and pure. His poetry was forceful, and his denunciations of priestly wealth and hypocrisy made him popular. He heard sutras in the sound of wind and water, and heaven's triumph over death in every moment of life which has conquered fear.[4]

The two sides of Zen are not wholly incompatible. Their interaction is evident in the famous Zen ox-herding pictures, a traditional series of allegorical paintings which have been interpreted by several different masters. They begin by showing a young man seeking out and taming an obstreperous ox, which represents the mind. He reaches the point where he can indifferently ride on the ox's back. Then the ox disappears, next the man, leaving only nature; finally all disappears to leave only the white circle of the Void. But in the last picture we see the seeker once again, now a jovial old man, utterly free of all inhibition or self-consciousness or dignity, dancing and playing with children in the road as he advances "with bliss-bearing hands" toward a city. Taming the ox was discipline— but its goal was to evoke the naturalness and unconstricted spontaneity of the Void itself by taking away everything, all fears and habits and concepts, which were not the pure "suchness" of original nature.

The same principle applies to Zen art. The contribution of the Zen spirit to the arts of East Asia is, as is well known, immensely rich and varied. There is a distinctive Zen style in painting, poetry, landscaping, the tea ceremony, even the martial arts. What characterizes all these diverse forms of expression is a simplicity and naturalism which appears effortless, but which finds just the right gesture to catch the essence of the moment it reflects through a direct, concentrated intuition resulting from deep inwardness and long discipline. Zen naturalness is not simply living by surface moods and feelings, which, according to Buddhism, are not "natural" at all but a tangled web woven of karma, suffering, and desire, compounded by ignorance. It is, rather, a ruthless pruning away of all these that allows the deep, true, and joyous spontaneity of one's buddhahood to well up. And because it had undistorted perception, this nature intuitively knows, and can flawlessly express through one's chosen medium, the true nature of all other things.

It is the sense of transcendent freedom from structures, whether of mind or society, and of seamless harmony with our ultimate environment, the infinite universe itself, which is suggested by this ideal that has most appealed to Westerners drawn to Zen. It is to these persons we must now turn.

Zen Mountaineering

We climaxed discussion of Theosophy with a single archetypal incident, Olcott's "instinctive act of pooja" in stooping down to kiss the ground upon landing at Bombay on February 16, 1879. Let us begin the discussion of American Zen with another symbolic date, October 22, 1955.

On that evening, the novelist Jack Kerouac and the poet Gary Snyder camped together in the High Sierras east of San Francisco. A third companion, John Montgomery, was following and camped below them.

It was a memorable evening. The high-country air was cool and fresh and more intoxicating than wine; the brilliant stars were as big and close as the stars of a fairy-tale world. Snyder, much the better outdoorsman, cooked a hearty supper. Then came talk, hours of the wonderful, ebullient camping talk of gifted young men, talk about everything under heaven: adventures, travels, women, poetry, philosophy. And Buddhism. For Kerouac and Snyder considered themselves Buddhists, after a fashion. Snyder was engaged in orientalist studies and was more advanced and serious than his friend in the faith of the Middle Way; Kerouac, having but recently turned to the Triple Refuge, regarded Snyder as his mentor.

But it was Jack Kerouac, chronicler of the 1950s "beat generation," who made the evening in the mountains famous. Although it is briefly described in Snyder's journal, it emerges as one of the unforgettable scenes in Kerouac's autobiographical novel *The Dharma Bums*.[5] That book is Kerouac's most famous work after his best-selling *On the Road;* it covers a year of his life in 1955–56 when he was close to Snyder, Allen Ginsberg, Kenneth Rexroth, and other lights of the "San Francisco Poetry Renaissance" of the late fifties. The basic theme of *The Dharma Bums* is Zen, or, more precisely, "Zen lunacy," and Gary Snyder, thinly disguised as Japhy Ryder, is the hero, the ideal youthful Zen enthusiast and adept.

Kerouac met Snyder through Ginsberg, whom Kerouac had known as far back as 1944, and who considered Snyder the most worthwhile person in the San Francisco scene. Their meeting was just before the legendary poetry reading in the Six Gallery in early October 1955, when the San Francisco Poetry Renaissance was allegedly born. Kenneth Rexroth was master of ceremonies, Allen Ginsberg first uttered his celebrated "Howl," Snyder delivered some lines on Coyote, the trickster-hero of the North American Indians, other young poets also read. About one hundred fifty people were present, and there was enough wine, raucous fun, and literary talk to last through dawn.

Kerouac devotes four freewheeling pages in *The Dharma Bums* to that epic night, but it was only the beginning of his relationship with Ryder/Snyder. The Japhy of the novel was living in Berkeley in a tiny cottage. He had been studying Japanese and Chinese at the university and on his own for three years, prepatory to going to a Zen monastery in Japan for further Zen practice the following year. That fall he was translating the Chinese Zen hermit-poet Han Shan, "Cold Mountain."

But Japhy was no mere scholar; he spent summers lumberjacking and fire-watching in the Northwest, and was as much at home in the mountains as amid Chinese and Japanese texts. Nor was he a rigorous ascetic; one could usually find women and cheap wine around his cabin, and it was the scene of some wild parties. But Japhy could be "tender as a mother" and quiet as a saint, and went his own way whenever you began to think you understood him. Over the whole narrative of *The Dharma Bums,* which focuses on his adamantine and mysterious holiness, lies knowledge that these boyish days are for him only an interlude and a preliminary; at the end of the year he will be going to his monastery in Japan. Something very deep and special set Japhy apart; all who met him, especially the immature but sensitive Kerouac, sensed that.

For one thing, he was always making simple gifts to people. On the mountain that mythic evening, Japhy gave Ray Smith (Kerouac) a worn Buddhist rosary—an act of *dana,* donation, one of the six Buddhist *paramitas* or perfections.

For another, he had that peculiar grace, "lightness," and air of physical and psychic balance which comes from great equilibrium and reserve strength on many levels, from knowing what the universe is and where one fits in it. The morning after they camped on the mountain, the pair pushed their way toward the peak. Kerouac lost his nerve, but Japhy ran like a mountain goat over the crags and through the fog to the peak. Then Smith (Kerouac) says, "Suddenly I heard a beautiful broken yodel of a strange musical and mystical intensity in the wind, and looked up, and it was Japhy standing on top of Matterhorn peak letting out his triumphant mountain-conquering Buddha Mountain Smashing song of Joy. It was beautiful."[6] (There is a Zen saying, "When you get to the top of a mountain, keep climbing.")

The Dharma Bums has its weaknesses as literature. The structure is limp and lacks consistency. Female characters are stereotypical mothers and waitresses, or "chicks" who appear out of nowhere for a party, then conveniently disappear when the menfolk get down to the serious business of drinking wine and discussing philosophy. As for Zen Buddhism, there is no evidence in the novel that Japhy or anyone else ever regularly practiced *zazen,* or were aware that it was an important part of the faith they loved to celebrate—though Smith/Kerouac did have a "nice old rocking chair" on the dilapidated porch of his house, where he liked to sit in the morning and read the Diamond Sutra, even as Thoreau had, we gather, read the "Bhagvat Geeta" some Walden morning. But whatever the gaps in the book's knowledge of Buddhism (and Kerouac would have been responsible for these, not Snyder), it was the anti-structural, spontaneous side of Zen that its heroes wished to celebrate—"Zen lunacy," they called it.

Moreover, the romantic, youthful exuberance of *The Dharma*

Bums manages to rise above its limitations and makes the book not only an important social document relevant to excursus religion in America, but also strangely moving. Above all, the figure of Japhy, elusive yet unforgettable, coarse yet pious, both American and oriental at once, both a Walt Whitman and a Han Shan, stays in one's mind. He remains unique, yet also archetypical, even as he was at the end of the book, when the physical Japhy was seven thousand miles away answering the sonorous meditation bell of an ancient temple, but the narrator, descending a mountain Japhy had loved, perceived some twisted gnarly trees:

> And suddenly it seemed I saw that unimaginable little Chinese bum standing there, in the fog, with that expressionless humor on his seamed face. It wasn't the real-life Japhy of rucksacks and Buddhism studies and big mad parties at Corte Madera, it was the realer-than-life Japhy of my dreams, and he stood there saying nothing. "Go away, thieves of the mind!" he cried down the hollows of the unbelievable Cascades.[7]

Jack Kerouac

Jean-Louis Kerouac (1922–69), called Jack, was born and raised in Lowell, Massachusetts. His family was French-Canadian, of Breton origin, and there is more than a little Celtic romanticism in his love of words, wandering, and magical glamor.

After a very indifferent Merchant Marine and Navy career during the war, and equally indifferent starts at college and odd jobs, Kerouac hitchhiked to the West Coast in 1947. That epic journey, together with later excursions to New Orleans and Mexico, was the basis of *On the Road,* the novel which ten years later was to make its author famous and financially secure, and which, for all its uncouthness, was a literary gust of fresh air that managed to catch the inchoate rebellion of a new postwar generation.

What is of most concern to us is how that rebellion got linked up with Zen Buddhism—so that for the "Dharma Bums," the rhetoric of the Eastern faith and the lifestyle of the "Zen lunatics" became both an expression and a legitimation of their dissatisfaction and their "hip" way of life.

Jack Kerouac was raised in a highly traditional French Catholic family. His mother, upon whom he was dependent and with whom he lived off and on all his life, was very devout. (Kerouac liked to say that his prose style came from his boyhood experience of making a full confession to a priest every week, cleansing himself of all he had done by giving a full account of it.)

But away from home, other things attracted him. In 1954, when he was feeling lost and low, he discovered Buddhism. He had actually come into contact with it the year before, when Allen Ginsberg, while studying Chinese painting, had read some of D. T. Suzuki's essays on Zen and talked to Jack about them. But Kerouac was unimpressed at the time. Then, in January of 1955, Kerouac moved in with Neal Cassady (Dean Moriarty in *On the Road*) and his family and began serious Buddhist study.

It started when Cassady expressed his enthusiasm for the American mystic Edgar Cayce, especially for his teachings regarding reincarnation, and Jack responded by arguing against him. Kerouac had shortly before reread Thoreau, whom he had long admired, and, recalling the Walden sage's citations of Hindu philosophy, had turned to Eastern texts. He rummaged through libraries to find books like a translation of Ashvagosha's life of the Buddha, and told Cassady that Cayce's literalistic idea of continuous reincarnations of an immortal soul was unsophisticated from a Buddhist point of view, since in the eyes of the great faith of East Asia there is really no ego, and so nothing to reincarnate and nothing to be immortal.

For himself, though, Kerouac prized most the first of the Buddha's Four Noble Truths: All Life is Suffering. To him this verity, uttered by one as quiet and deep as the World-Enlightened One, gave some perspective on his own confused and tormented life—with his restlessness, his apparent failure (he was not yet successful as a writer), his second ex-wife's taking him to court to win child support, his pointless appetites for drink and drugs.

By late in 1954 he had taken up Mahayana literature, especially the *Diamond Sutra*, with its lines like these:

> All composite things
> Are like a dream, a phantasm, a
>   bubble, and a shadow,
> Are like a dew-drop and a flash of lightning;
> They are thus to be regarded.

He had decided he was going to become a bodhisattva and painfully practiced meditation briefly every day. He wrote several hundred pages, called *Some of the Dharma* (never published, though he tried) of notes and reflections on his new faith. Kerouac went back East for Christmas 1954, and stayed through the following summer; his shiftlessness and his Buddhism aggravated his prosaic relatives and led to some stormy living room scenes. But in mid-summer he unexpectedly got word that *On the Road*, many times rejected by publishers, had been accepted by Viking Press. Jubilant and with an advance in his pocket, he went to Mexico City, did some writing, and then returned to California, where he hopped a freight out of Los Angeles to the Bay Area, a journey immortalized in the opening scene of *The Dharma Bums*. Next came the great Six Gallery reading and the meeting with Snyder, who deepened and stabilized the novelist's Buddhism.[8]

Several observations can be appended to this precis of how Jack Kerouac came to Buddhism. First, we note the indirect influence through Ginsberg of D. T. Suzuki (1870–1966), that Japanese scholar who produced an almost endless series of books and essays in English on Zen. Although there were other influences, the Western vogue for Zen would have been almost inconceivable without Suzuki. He and those influenced by him have given Zen more English-language literature than all the rest of Buddhism put together. No doubt this gave Zen an edge in the spiritual market-place, though it is probably true that no other form of Buddhism could have had the Western cultural impact of Zen, with its conceptual flexibility and its easy-to-appreciate art. Suzuki made the transmission process all the easier by stressing an interpretation of Zen which drew on Western existentialism at the expense of the discipline, cultic, and sociological sides of Zen in Japan, mixing in just enough of the latter to give it an excitingly exotic flavor but not enough to intimidate the adventurous spirit. Suzuki was himself no holy, unworldly monk; he was a layman and a highly sophisticated student of Western thought who knew how to present Zen to make it a live option in the Euro-American context. Nor was he unaware of the Western tradition of alternative spirituality within which Zen was to fit; it is curious to note that there is a 1914 Japanese translation of Swedenborg's *New Jerusalem* by D. T. Suzuki, who did several such works on commission for the Swedenborgian church.

Second, we may note the role of Thoreau in first directing Kerouac's attention to Eastern thought. The seminal importance of the New England Transcendentalists and their spiritual kin, like Whitman, in shaping the American experience of excursus religion can hardly be overemphasized, as we have seen. Kerouac read Henry Thoreau several times in an attempt to get into the side of the American dream Walden represented; he had always wanted to go somewhere and live the Walden life. Instead he discovered Thoreau's East.

Third, the discovery of Buddhism came in the midst of discussions about emergent tradition figures and ideas—namely, Edgar Cayce and reincarnation. Buddhism emerged as an option when the language, sociology, and conceptual frame of reference was already defined by talk of alternatives to normative religion, and of the pre-existence and destiny of the soul. We have already observed that Cayce's doctrines were probably borrowed from Theosophy.

Fourth and most important, Kerouac became serious about Buddhism following a self-alienation from American values, above all from the apotheosis of surburbia of those Eisenhower years, as exemplified by his wandering and seemingly unproductive life. The example of another American dropout, Thoreau, was not enough as his personal troubles mounted, though the earlier writer's Hindu citations pointed in the right direction. But Kerouac's inner compass was far more wobbly indeed than the old-fashioned New England conscience of his model, his view of himself and the world correspondingly less sunny. He needed more than pantheism; he needed also the Buddha's clear-sighted diagnosis of the painful disease called separate existence. It was, then, after a prior state of essential alienation from America and inner despair that Kerouac was able to take refuge in the alternative from the East, and to read signposts to it in America's past. It is this process which both veils and reveals the fundamental continuity of emergent religion.

It must be noted that Kerouac's Buddhism did not wear particularly well. He was a falling star which quickly burned out, and the pitiful last decade of his life was marked by a desperation and incapacity which the bottle and life with mother seemed to solace better than the Dharma. But the significance of *The Dharma Bums,* both as symbol and influence, is not erased by this end. We

must now turn to him who, in the novel, Kerouac acknowledges is
ahead of him in the Buddha-stream, and observe how his career is
also a paradigm of Zen in the West.

Gary Snyder

Gary Snyder was born in San Francisco in 1930, but grew up amid
considerable poverty on a dairy farm in Washington state. He loved
the Pacific Northwest, with its towering mountains and dark forests, and early acquired a deep and romantic appreciation for wood-
craft and Native American lore unsullied by conventional religion.
He was not personally influenced by Theosophy in his turning to
Eastern or archaic American spiritual symbols. In 1942 he moved
with his family to Portland, Oregon, and there he graduated in
1951 from Reed College with majors in anthropology and literature. His most intense interest at the time was the mythology and
anthropology of the Amerindians who lived amid the woods and
mountains he loved.

In 1952 he moved to San Francisco and worked at various jobs
there. In 1953 he moved again to Berkeley, where he lived in the
little cottage described by Kerouac in *The Dharma Bums* and
studied Chinese and Japanese in the Department of Oriental Languages at the University of California in Berkeley, without neglect-
ing breaks to return to the forests and mountains. During summers
he made some money in logging and manning a fire lookout in
national forests—readers of *The Dharma Bums* will recall that, at
the end of the epic year therein transcribed, when Snyder left for
Japan, he got Kerouac/Smith the lookout job in Washington's Mt.
Baker National Forest that he had filled with mystical perfection a
season or two before.[9]

Snyder became increasingly involved with the East as well as with
ancient America. He says he was first drawn to the Far East by an
appreciation of Chinese poetry and the philosophy of Taoism, and
became interested in Zen when he realized that the spirit of philosophical Taoism survived in it. He first learned of Zen from the
works of D. T. Suzuki. He was also attracted to India by the
powerful archetypes of Hindu mythology; through the study of
Indian thought he perceived the richness of Indian Buddhist phi-

losophy and followed it from the original Mahayana systems to Zen.

He wrote poetry on Amerindian myths, seeing American lore in the crisp clarity of Zen perception. Not content with mere romantic appreciation of the Eastern school, he proceeded to ground himself in Zen through appropriate language skills and disciplined training. He translated, as we have seen, the poems of that kindred soul of a dozen centuries before, Han-Shan (Kanzan in Japanese, literally "Cold Mountain.")

He began the published version of the Cold Mountain Poems with a preface by the hermit-poet's contemporary, Lu Ch'iu-yin, governor of T'ai prefecture, who said, "No one knows just what sort of man Han-Shan was." He was a mountain madman, who looked like a tramp, "yet in every word he breathed was a meaning in line with the subtle principles of things if only you thought of it deeply."[10] Kerouac, at least, read Gary Snyder to be the same kind of man.

It was in the fall of 1955, then, that Gary Snyder met Kerouac through Ginsberg, just before the legendary poetry reading at the Six Galley. In May of 1956 he left for Japan on a scholarship provided by the First Zen Institute of America, in New York, to study Zen and Japanese in Kyoto. His patron and teacher in Japan was Ruth Fuller Sasaki, doyenne of American Zen. He stayed in the Japanese Zen temple a year and a half, then, in 1958, worked his way back to America on a ship. He returned to Japan in 1959, studying under Oda Sesso Roshi, head abbot of the famous Dai-toku temple in Kyoto, and for a while afterward alternated between living in Japan, working at sea, and publishing his poetry and giving poetry readings in America. In 1961-62 he traveled in India, visiting Hindu and Buddhist holy places. He now lives in the foothills of the Sierra Nevadas with his wife, Masa, and two sons. In the seventies he was involved in environmentalist thought and politics, and served as a member of the California Arts Council, appointed by the governor.

The length of time he has spent in Japanese temples certainly confirms the seriousness about Zen of this paragon of Zen-American mysticism. Yet it is important to note that he is just as authentically a successor of the American radical tradition often related earlier to Transcendentalism, Spiritualism, and Theosophy. There is the same anarchistic protest, the same deep feeling for the heritage of the American Indians and their spirituality, mixed with the same—or a similar—thirst for an appropriate exoticism which would confirm and complete one's sense of being both more profoundly and spiritually American than most others, and yet not at home in conventional American society. As with them, the quest for excursus into the archaic led to an excursus to the distant and exotic: the past and the far away became almost one. In 1961 Snyder wrote: "As a poet I hold the most archaic values on earth. They go back to the late Paleolithic: the fertility of the soil, the magic of animals, the power-vision in solitude, the terrifying initiation and rebirth, the love and ecstasy of the dance, the common work of the tribe."[11]

Yet all of this was not wholly inconsistent with the great Eastern religions; later Snyder pointed out that Buddhism and Hinduism carry much of Stone Age religion with them in such practices as shaving the head.[12] The most important product of his experiences is the rich kaleidoscope of his major prose book, *Earth House Hold*, which can move from vignettes of a very "tight" sesshin, or intensive meditation session, at the Shokokuji in Kyoto, to experiments with living a primitive life on an island with his Japanese wife, to accounts of the racy conversation of a tanker crew.

In 1975 Gary Snyder received the Pulitzer Prize in poetry for his book *Turtle Island*. Its poems are ostensibly drawn largely from native American mythology, though more subtly they reflect a biological systems-theory of ecology, and the theme of the interdependence of all beings supremely expressed, as Snyder has himself emphasized, in the Buddhist Avatamsaka or Garland Sutra.[13] In a prose afterword, the poet speaks of his Zen training as a major formative influence.

Alan Watts

During his San Francisco and Berkeley days, Gary Snyder was familiar with the American Academy of Asian Studies in San Francisco, though he never formally studied at it. This institution was organized in 1951 by Frederick Spiegelberg, and was oriented toward a serious but accessible communication of Asian culture to the general public. The Academy played an indefinable but not insignificant role in shaping the "San Francisco Renaissance" of the fifties, with its Zen interests, and the even more explosive Asiaticism of the sixties "counterculture," whose mecca was San Francisco's Haight-Ashbury district. As much as anything, this was because one of the Academy's leading teachers in the fifties was a middle-aged Englishman named Alan Watts (1915–73), a good friend of Snyder's.

Generously and gracefully, Alan Watts in his autobiography disclaims credit for Gary Snyder and says that Kerouac's characterization of him as Japhy Ryder "hardly begins to do him justice." Watts adds that Snyder studied Chinese at the University of California and Zen in Kyoto, "but when I am dead I would like to be able to say that he is carrying on everything I hold most dearly, though with a different style. To put it in another way, my only regret is that I cannot formally claim him as my spiritual successor. He did it all on his own, but nevertheless he *is* just exactly what I have been trying to *say*." The supreme tribute is perhaps this: "I can only say that a universe which has manifested Gary Snyder could never be called a failure."[14]

Nonetheless, we cannot think of Gary Snyder's generation, and of Zen in America, without putting Alan Watts in the foreground. If Snyder *is* what he *says*, what Watts said has been immensely important to millions, as it was to Snyder himself.

Watts was a very different sort of man from Kerouac and Snyder. The genius of the latter two, in their different ways, was to make Zen appear a natural consummation and interpretive paradigm for that authentically American lifestyle and literary tradition represented by Thoreau, Whitman, and Tom Wolfe. Their Zen fitted like a glove to the way of that very American type, or at least ideal: the young man who thinks deeply but cares little for "success" or social grace, and, like a pilgrim-monk of old, wanders about in shabby clothes, logging, seafaring, hitchhiking, writing verse, and exulting in nature and the infinite. Gentle yet fiercely independent and vaguely radical, he is Johnny Appleseed, the young Frederick Evans, Henry Olcott after he carried the style to India, Gary Snyder, and many others. This lifestyle is deeply intertwined with excursus religion and is of sufficient and authentic cultural importance in

America that its latter-day interpenetration with imported Zen is highly significant and serves to help legitimate Zen both as American and as spiritually viable.

Alan Watts's role in the Zen movement was different from theirs, but had some inner continuities with their experience. Despite his very important position as a catalyst and interpreter, Watts was always in some deep, mainly inner sense an outsider to everything. He was more than a little alienated by British church and society as a young man, yet rootless as a transplanted Englishman in America, where his British public-school accent and manner sometimes put people off as being incongruous for a guru, and where (like many others in a similar situation) he sometimes overplayed the part. He was, after D. T. Suzuki, the West's foremost exponent of Zen, yet he never formally indentified himself with any Zen movement and did not call himself a Buddhist or anything else, nor did he practice meditation more than sporadically.

Despite the fact that Watts had only qualified enthusiasm for Kerouac's "beat Zen," there were certain odd parallels and paradoxes between his life and the French-Canadian's. Both were relatively short-lived; both originated as definite outsiders to the West Coast mysticism scene, and later became eminent stimulators and interpreters of it; both were prolific writers, with marvelous gifts of image and metaphor, who, in two paragraphs, could entice a reader into their worlds of fantasy or mystical reality through sheer word-wizardry, but who finally lacked a countervailing breadth (both men essentially say and do the same thing in all their books) or a capacity for tight literary discipline and intellectual rigor. Both men, moreover, for all their mysticism, lived personal lives which could scarcely be characterized as ascetic, and they made no secret of this in their autobiographical works (Watts's *In My Own Way;* virtually the whole corpus of Kerouac).

Paradox, though, is close to the center of meaning in the life of Alan Watts. That life was always something of a pendulum swinging between what we have here called established and emergent religion; nor did the pendulum stop when he ostensibly cut all ties with establishment, for he soon became so prominent a writer and spokesman for the other side as to become virtually an establishment in himself.

Watts was born in an English village, and grew up with a love for
the beautiful countryside of that land—a love like that of another
figure we have met in these pages, Frederick Evans of the Shakers.
There is little further parallel with the earlier emigrant, though.

Watts, though he did not attend university, acquired a solid
education at one of the best public schools, King's College in
Canterbury. In school, and during a few years afterward, when he
was, owing to his family's inability to afford formal higher education for him, "his own univerity," the bright young man discovered Buddhism and other exotic spiritual disciplines. In London,
during the dark years of the late thirties, he sought out book-
stores and circles of people interested in these disciplines. When
only twenty, he published his first book, *The Spirit of Zen*.

Christmas Humphreys, a London solicitor, Theosophist, and
Buddhist, took the young man under his wing and gave him an
unusual education in the spiritual mysteries of the East. He introduced him to the writings of D. T. Suzuki as early as 1930,
although Watts did not meet his great mentor in Zen until 1936.

Daisetz Teitaro Suzuki, whose influence on Kerouac and Snyder
we have already noted, first came to the West as early as 1897, when
his teacher, Soyen Roshi, arranged for him to become an editor of
the Open Court Publishing Company in LaSalle, Illinois. There he
remained as a guest of the distinguished publisher, Paul Carus,
until 1909, writing books, articles, and translations on Buddhism
and related topics. After he returned to Japan, he became a professor of English and married an American lady, Beatrice Lane, a
Buddhist scholar and writer of some importance herself, and, as we
have seen, an active Theosophist. On his way back to America in
1936, he attended a World Congress of Faiths in London, when
Watts met him. In 1950-58 he was again in America, teaching and
lecturing at universities, and the intense intellectual interest in Zen
of those days can be largely traced to this activity and to the
lingering influence of his earlier writing. Many Westerners came to
Zen through such books of his as *An Introduction to Zen Buddhism, Essays in Zen Buddhism, The Training of the Zen Buddhist
Monk, Manual of Zen Buddhism, Zen and Japanese Culture*.

Alan Watts was to have an interlude of a few years, however,
before he fulfilled the commission Suzuki might be supposed to

have given him. In 1938 he married, in an Anglican parish church in London, the daughter of a very wealthy Chicago businessman. Despite the establishment locale of the wedding, both partners were more or less Buddhist; the bride's mother was Ruth Fuller Everett, a leader in the First Zen Institute in New York. Indeed, after becoming widowed a few years later, this lady was to become well-known in her own right as a Zen writer and priest.

On the eve of World War II, Alan and Eleanor Watts came to New York. He immediately began the only kind of life with which he was ever happy or, for that matter, successful: an informal mixture of writing, teaching, and lecturing. He also maintained a close relationship with the Zen Institute.

However, drawn by the aesthetic appeal of Anglo-Catholicism and by a desire for a professional vocation in which he could fulfill within the context of his culture his main interest, religion, he determined to enter the priesthood of the Episcopal Church. On Ascension Day, 1945, Alan Watts was ordained in Chicago and became Episcopal chaplain at Northwestern University.

Five years later he was to leave the priesthood. But during those five years he constructed a ministry and a Christian theological style worth remembering. Indeed, his five brief years in the Episcopal Church and on the Northwestern campus were so highly charged that those in both institutions whose memories go back that far have little trouble remembering that brilliant, intense, loquacious, and flamboyant presence among them, who never lacked for money (his wife's), wit, or attention. Canterbury House under him was a virtually nonstop bull-session; his services drew worshipers from near and far to a rich liturgical splendor embellished with a sense of playfulness and to the incomparable mystical sermons of he who then as later could induce with words a sense of spiritual experience and of being on the "inside" of some cosmic secret.

Theologically he was still wrestling with the reconciliation of Buddhism and Christianity. In a book like *Behold the Spirit* (1947), deriving from this Christian period, he expounded a Christianity based on a pantheistic view of deity reinforced by both Eastern and Western mystical philosophies, but profoundly incarnational and sacramental in its mundane expression, and imbued with a deep appreciation of the spiritual significance of aesthetics and play. His next book, *The Supreme Identity* (1950), moved further in assimilating Eastern and Western paths to knowing the One in the Eternal Now—the one thing worth knowing, though uncontainable in words; *The Supreme Identity* is probably Watts's most substantial work as far as scholarship and sustained, serious philosophical discourse are concerned.

By the time it was published, Watts's career as a Christian priest was about over. He was in trouble for teaching libertarian views on sex and marriage; his own marriage was on the rocks; and his inner doubts concerning Christianity and his clerical calling could not be resolved. It became evident that the ministry was not for him and, despite his success as a university chaplain, he could not go on. He later wrote of the difference between the shaman and priest, the latter being an institutional officer and the former a loner who originates rather than follows traditions; he was all shaman. In the summer of 1950 his marriage and his ministry ended.

He was on his own at thirty-five, for the first time in his life without money, profession, or social role. It was a difficult passage, even a sort of initiation. He landed on his feet the next year, though. He remarried, and was appointed to the faculty of the American Academy of Asian Studies in San Francisco.

For the rest of his life, apart from the few years of full-time teaching at the American Academy, Watts was again doing what he liked best, and very successfully: scrambling to make a life and a living from writing, holding seminars, lecturing, finagling grants, being a celebrity. A three-year fellowship from the Bollengen Foundation enabled him to do research for the book most relevant to our purpose, *The Way of Zen*, published in 1957. But his numerous other books, including such well-known titles as *Beyond Theology, Erotic Spirituality, The Wisdom of Insecurity, This is It,* and *The Two Hands of God,* culminating in his autobiography, *In My Own Way,* testify to his literary virtuosity. (His father wrote the introduction to the last, which, as Watts remarks, must be a unique literary phenomenon.) Apart from the divide between his Christian and post-Christian phases, however, one detects a curious lack of movement or development on a deep level, although there are superficial tie-ins with passing vogues: Zen in the fifties, psychedelia in the sixties. But all the way through there are the same attacks on the Judeo-Christian God the Father, the same Krishna-murtian intentional intentionlessness, the same Zen/Vedanta pantheistic glow. It is all said eloquently, and said over and over.

Nonetheless, *The Way of Zen* remains the most accessible general introduction to Zen in English, at least in the D. T. Suzuki manner of interpretation, and as such has been immensely influential. The tone of Watts's approach is captured by the opening sentence: "Zen Buddhism is a way and a view of life which does not belong to any of the formal categories of modern Western thought."[15] The hard monastic discipline side of Zen is glossed over, but we are immediately intrigued by what doubtless intrigues most Westerners when they first turn to the contemplation of Zen: the idea of a whole new "view of life" and one so unique it cannot even be handled by the mental machinery we have used thus far. Watts properly does not overdo the "mysterious East" business, but he does emphasize that Zen and even *zazen* are more an attitude or kind of awareness than a particular practice; this he got from Suzuki, whom he says elsewhere was really more Taoist than Japanese Zen. Watts liked the free inwardness he associated with true Taoism and Zen, and disdained the "skinhead military zip" of many Japanese monks. Gary Snyder had some good things to say about Suzuki and Watts:

> The reason people criticize Suzuki is that there almost aren't enough words to say how big he was. What other Japanese person has had so much influence on the world at large? We don't think of it that way because we take him to be so much our own, but he is Japan's greatest cultural contribution to the world so far. In Europe and America he has influenced everything—psychology, music, aesthetics, architecture, landscape design—and through his disciples like Christmas Humphreys, Edward Conze, Hubert Benoit, Bernard Phillips, John Cage, and Alan Watts, he has permeated all levels of society. He has been the catalyst of some real social changes, in attitudes towards the self, towards effort, towards involvement, in attitudes on the nature of creativity, on the value of verbalization and articulation as against the intuitive approach. All these things which are not 'pure Zen' or Zen practice are nonetheless very important humanly. You can say about Alan Watts's books that they have done a lot of people a lot of good in terms of turning down their anxiety, and in stimulating them towards a more creative attitude towards themselves. Whether or not his books are 'real Zen' is beside the point. You meet people all the time

who say, 'I owe so much to Alan Watts's writings. They helped me lead
my life.' And that is how great Suzuki is. He is more than just a part
of bringing Zen to the West. He entered deeply into new social attitudes in the world.[16]

Formal Zen

Thus far most of what we have discussed of Zen is in the nature of
diffuse cultural influence or persons mainly responsible for that
influence. Probably that is the most significant feature of Zen: its
ability to suggest, in Watts's phrase, "a view of life which does not
belong to any of the formal categories of modern Western
thought." Zen's putatively supplemental or noncompetitive relation to Western thought, and even to Western religion, is essential
to its role in the ecology of American culture and to the understanding of emergent and excursus religion. But it is also important
to see the place of the formal Zen centers, such as the First Zen
Institute of America in New York, significant at one point, as we
have seen, in the career of Alan Watts. Excursus religion tends to
avoid direct competition with established religion, but maintains
interpersonal relationships among its followers either more diffuse
or more intense than those found in mainline churches; we now
move to consider those Zen relationships, centering around that of
roshi or master and disciple, but also sometimes involving community, that can be very intense.

This is, of course, the story of those Zen priests (not laymen like
Suzuki) who have come to America to live and teach Zen in a
formal manner. The tale begins with the redoubtable Soyen Shaku
(1859-1919), a Japanese monk who wrote of himself in 1888:

> This fellow was a son of Nobusuke Goemon Ichenose of Takahama,
> the province of Wakasa. His nature was stupid and tough. When he
> was young, none of his relatives liked him. When he was twelve years
> old, he was ordained as a monk by Ekkei, Abbot of Myo-shin Monas-
> tery. Afterwards, he studied literature under Shungai of Kennin Monas-
> tery for three years, and gained nothing. Then he went to Mii-dera and
> studied Tendai philosophy under Tai-ho for a summer, and gained
> nothing. After this, he went to Bizen and studied Zen under the old
> teacher Gisan for one year, and attained nothing. He then went to the
> East, to Kamakura, and studied under the Zen master Ko-sen in the

Engaku Monastery for six years, and added nothing to the aforesaid nothingness. He was in charge of a little temple, Butsu-nichi, one of the temples of the Engaku Cathedral, for one year and from there he went to Tokyo to attend Kej-o College for one year and a half, making himself the worst student there; and forgot the nothingness that he had gained. Then he created for himself new delusions, and came to Ceylon in the spring of 1887; and now, under the Ceylon monk he is studying the Pali language and Hinayana Buddhism. Such a wandering mendicant! He ought to repay the twenty years of debts to those who fed him in the name of Buddhism.[17]

This fellow (and those who know something of Zen philosophy will catch the double meaning of the nothingness he attained and forgot) did something to repay those debts when, in 1893, he came to the United States to attend the World Parliament of Religions, a conference that was seminal to the Easternization of emergent religion in America in several respects. Like Swami Vivekananda, the founder of the Ramakrishna Mission and the Vedanta Societies in the West, Soyen found that the 1893 event kindled something in the West; it was a moment at the height of imperialism when its reverse side, the penetration of the conqueror by the conquered, began to show itself for those who had eyes to see.

Soyen returned to Japan and taught Zen in Kamakura after the parliament. Among his students were D. T. Suzuki and Nyogen Senzaki (1876–1958). Soyen came to America a second time in 1905, when he was the guest of Mr. and Mrs. Alexander Russell of San Francisco; Mrs. Russell was the first American to study the Zen "riddles" or *koans* formally. Senzaki came to America the same year. He was the first Zen monk to reside permanently in this country. His life after his arrival at age twenty-nine was typical of that of the Japanese immigrant of those days. He worked as a houseboy, cook, waiter, and finally teacher of the Japanese language, and did not begin lecturing on Buddhism until he had been in America for twenty years. But he then devoted more than thirty more years to mission work, and during this time (except for the war years, when he was interned) he taught in *zendos* in San Francisco and Los Angeles, and through his students was responsible for Zen centers from New York to Hawaii.

Senzaki acquainted himself with the American intellectual heritage, and was surprised to find what he considered an excellent preparation for Zen in the American freethinkers, from Thomas Paine to Robert Ingersoll, and in Ralph Waldo Emerson. Above all, though, he believed that the pragmatism of William James was but the Zen of another culture, ''another name for one manifestation of the sparkling rays of Zen in the actual, practical world.'' Surely, he thought, people with the rationality, informality, pragmatism, simplicity, and love of nature of Americans will not forever be able to resist the appeal of Zen.[18]

Another influential personality was Sokatsu Shaku Roshi (1869–1954), also a student of Soyen, who came to America with six disciples in 1906. They bought a farm in Hayward, California, and when it failed, established a Zen center in San Francisco. In 1910 they returned to Japan, leaving only one member of the party behind, Shigemitsu Sasaki, who was later to become the *roshi* of the First Zen Institute of America in New York, a teacher of Alan Watts, and the husband of Ruth Fuller Sasaki.

In February, 1911, Sasaki crossed the Shasta mountains on foot; he finally reached the Rogue River Valley and stayed with a friend there, meditating daily on a big rock by the stream. He led a wandering life for several years and ended up in New York. There he lived in Greenwich Village and got to know some of the ''bohemian'' poets of the day. He returned to Japan in 1919 to complete his study of Zen, but came back to New York in 1928 to promulgate Zen there, and in 1930 Sasaki (his monastic name was Sokei-an) founded the First Zen Institute, then the Buddhist Society. The most prominent of his American followers included Mary Farkas and Ruth Fuller Everett, whom he later married, and who was to become Watts's mother-in-law.

In passing, we must note the almost uncanny parallel between Sasaki's life as a lonely Zen priest in the America of the World War I era, and that of the ''dharma bums'' of American Zen some forty years later. Here is the same Zen mountaineering in the rich, meditative woods of the Northwest, and the same interaction with the alienated urban poets of the day. Already Zen had established a relationship with the perennial American themes of understanding spiritually the fabulous natural splendor of the land, so majestic as almost to mock the Puritan concept of cosmic fallenness, and to the inner malaise of the person of fine poetic and intellectual sensitivity in this land of supposed materialistic crassness.

In 1941 the Institute tried to begin a new work in a new building owned by Ruth Everett on East 65th Street. The new Institute was opened on December 7th, 1941—and shortly after was swarming with FBI men. Sasaki was interned in 1942. His health failed; in 1943 he was released but was able to do little. In 1944, partly to stabilize the Institute's legal position in the difficult wartime situation and partly (according to Gary Snyder) out of love, Sasaki and the widowed Ruth Everett were married. In 1945 Sasaki Roshi died.

In the postwar decades, when the American mood turned suddenly from a chauvinistic antipathy toward all things Japanese to an equally uncritical enthusiasm for them, as occupation GIs came back with wondrous tales of the land of kimonos and courtesy, the Zen Institute flourished. Our attention, however, must turn to one whose orientalism was older and deeper, and whose impact on American Zen is incalculable, Sasaki's widow, Ruth Fuller Sasaki.

Ruth Fuller Sasaki (1893–1967) first learned about Zen in 1930, when she visited D. T. Suzuki on the way back from a trip to China. Her earlier college studies in Sanskrit and Pali had, however, given her a background valuable for understanding Buddhism. Two years later she returned to Japan to study at a Zen monastery for three and a half months. In 1938 she settled in New York and became, with her ample financial means, the principal supporter of the Institute.

The most remarkable phase of her life, however, came after the war. Beginning a new life as a serious scholar and Zen adept at over fifty years of age, she came to Japan, where she lived for the remainder of her life, studying under the abbot of the great Daitokuji in Kyoto. In time she rebuilt and became priest herself of a dilapidated temple within the Daitokuji complex, the first Westerner to hold such a position. In this capacity and as leader of the First Zen Institute of America in Kyoto she befriended the many foreigners, including Gary Snyder, who came to Japan in the fifties and sixties hoping to study Zen. It was here also that she wrote several important scholarly monographs and translations, and her excellent book *Zen Dust* (with Miura Roshi). Indeed, one of her most valuable contributions was her insistence upon solid Zen scholarship, which contrasts with the attitude of the more artless Western Zennist. She had a mastery of Japanese and classical Chinese, and an ability in Sanskrit, Pali, and European languages, equal to that of any academic savant. Her Zen was far removed from the "beat" style of Kerouac (though, oddly, it shared the same capacity for deracination and the linking figure of Gary Snyder); the Zen of her erstwhile son-in-law Alan Watts perhaps lay midway between the two.

More Zen

Several disciplic lineages from major teachers, both those we have discussed and a few others, have entered American Zen. Most are interrelated, going back to the previously discussed Soyen Shaku, to his teacher Imakita Kosen, and ultimately to the great Ekaku Hakuin in the eighteenth century, who developed the present system of *koan* study and who, indeed, virtually created modern Rinzai Zen.[19]

There is another tradition, however, the Harada lineage, and it is Soto, the other major school of Zen besides Rinzai. (Rinzai has emphasized *koan* study, while Soto has emphasized Zen sitting.) The great modern figure of the Harada lineage was Hakuun Yasutani (1885–1973), who, like Harada, actually combined both Soto and Rinzai techniques. His most influential American disciple was Philip Kapleau, who first came to Japan in 1946 as a reporter in the war crimes trials. (Many are the Americans in Zen and other Eastern spiritual movements who first met the Orient amid the storm and glory of war and occupation.) In 1951 he attended D. T. Suzuki's lectures at Columbia University. In 1953 he went to Japan, searching for a teacher, coming in time to Harada and his student Yasutani. When he returned to America in 1966, he established an important Zen center in Rochester, New York.

Kapleau's book *The Three Pillars of Zen* (1965), based on Yasutani's teaching, has undoubtedly been one of the most influential Western books on Zen, after those of Suzuki and Watts. It is, in fact, a good corrective to the latter two, for it emphasizes the importance of Zen sitting and the traditional relation of *roshi* and student. Its detailed accounts of Zen experience by both Western and Japanese practitioners make it an important document for the psychology of religion.

The largest American Zen center is the San Francisco Zen Center.

Interestingly, it is not itself related to either the Kosen or Harada lineages, but began in a different manner. Its effectual founder and first *roshi* was Shunryu Suzuki (1904-71), the son of a Soto priest, and himself priest of an important temple in Japan at only thirty-one years of age. In 1959 he unexpectedly came to America to serve as priest of a Japanese-American Soto temple in San Francisco. So great was the interest in Zen in the community, and so effective his spiritual charisma, that an informal body of occidental disciples gathered around Suzuki; this group was incorporated in 1962 as the Zen Center. It flourished in the sixties, developing several branches in the Bay area. Headquartered now in a fifty-room building in downtown San Francisco, where many residential Zen students live, it also operates Green Gulch Farm near Sausalito and the famous and spectacularly located Zen Mountain Center, dedicated to intensive training, at Tassajara Hot Springs in the mountains behind Carmel. When Suzuki Roshi died in 1971, he was succeeded by an American *roshi,* Richard Baker.[20]

The Zen Center is typical of the groups we are discussing in that its membership is both intense and often short-term; it is largely residential, and many members (even if not residential) practice *zazen* up to twice a day, a level of participation far closer to that of the Christian, or Buddhist, monk than of the ordinary churchgoer. Yet in 1970 a leading officer estimated the dropout rate to be about 80 percent a year. He adds that many students who survive the first year seem to drop out in the third, which appears to be a difficult one that involves a major adjustment; Zen students of four years or more, though, may be considered senior and stable.[21] However, the center has since become much more stable, which is characteristic of the equilibrium reached in the seventies of many new spiritual movements that had their starts in the sixties.

The other ten or twelve American Zen centers established after the Korean War and after the Zen enthusiasms of the fifties have explored diverse ways of practicing Zen on these shores. The Rinzai-related Cimarron Zen Center in Los Angeles sponsors the austere Mt. Baldy Center deep in the California mountains, which is probably more like a strict Japanese Zen monastery in discipline and practice than any other establishment in this country. The Sotoist Mt. Shasta Zen Center, under the direction of Jiyu Kennett, an Englishwoman who is a Zen *roshi,* has experimented with such Westernizing techniques as chanting the sutras in English plainsong.

On the other end of the scale, the general cultural influence of Zen continues apace. In 1974 Robert M. Pirsig's remarkable *Zen and the Art of Motorcycle Maintenance* made the best-seller lists and, while there is not much Zen in it once one gets past the title, it is a rich philosophical novel. The popularity of the title and the semi-autobiographical content shows that the Kerouac tradition of making the word Zen serve as shorthand for the values of the American spiritual picaresque, in which cross-country travel by alienated intellectuals goes with self-discovery and Whitmanesque unfolding of the spiritual meaning of America, is far from dead. It may even be becoming a genre. Whatever purists may say, Zen is a useful label, for, by the exoticism of its reference, it serves to distinguish the picaresque—which is an excursus of the spirit— from that other American genre, the Dos Passos or Erskine Caldwell wandering in which one is always at home, celebrating or vexing the too familiar. In any case, there is Zen precedent for the wanderer —Basho in Japan and Soyen Shaku in America—as well as for the still meditator, and also for Zennists like Gary Snyder and Ruth Fuller Sasaki, who represent both Zen roles.

Then there is Zen as spiritual excursus for those already within a circle of faith. We can only allude to books like Dom Aelred Graham, *Zen Catholicism* (1963), Thomas Merton, *Mystics and Zen Masters* (1967), and William Johnston, *The Still Point* (1970), as evidence of a burgeoning, and thus far mostly Roman Catholic, dialogue between Christianity and Zen. These are writers familiar with the Christian mystical tradition of Dionysius, Eckhart, the *Cloud of Unknowing,* and John of the Cross; the parallels and differences, especially of theological interpretation, have for them and for many of their readers proved a deep well of creative insight. If the day is past when Christian thinkers can work just in terms of their own tradition and its interaction with Western thought, as Cantwell Smith has suggested, and if the next great burst of theological work will come from dialogue with the world religions, then the foundations are already being laid in the case of Zen.[22] But it is significant to note that most of this writing is basically in response to D. T. Suzuki's presentation of Zen to the West; the initiative for dialogue, in other words, came from Zen.

Still another example of Zen in America may be the Erhard Seminars Training, or "est," a mind-improvement process which by the late seventies had graduated well over 100,000 Americans. Werner Erhard, the founder and leader, acknowledges that some Zen training was important in his development of the est idea, as was reading Alan Watts, although it was certainly not the only influence—he was also involved in Scientology, Silva Mind Control, humanistic psychology, and many other current "self-actualization" techniques. Est might, in fact, be considered a sort of ultimate, demythologized simplification and rationalization of the whole popular self-tranformation process into a few easy steps and concepts (or rather non-concepts). It could be seen as the ultimate Americanization of Zen, for, as far as I can see, the gist of it is Zen, but the language is wholly American—as is the junior executive atmosphere of the seminars—and there are no exotic trappings.

Like one of Kerouac's dharma bums, except for his background as a successful businessman, Erhard got his basic insight, he says, while driving south on highway 101 in California. He directly experienced his self, and no longer identified it with his body or personality or past or future or feelings or thought or circumstances or self-image—and he realized that verbalization is irrelevant.[23]

All this, very Zen indeed, is what the seminars communicate, and through such Zen-like techniques as quiet sitting and working inwardly on *koan*-like questions which (to use est terms) probe the "barriers" that maintain our "belief systems" and keep us from being "at the cause" of our "experience"—for only "experience," so easily obscured by "considerations" (value systems, judgments) and "chatter" and the space/time illusions we mistake for "reality," is the true source of awareness. "Getting" this is to "get clear" and be "at the cause" of one's experience rather than "at its effect."

This very diverse panorama, from lonely prewar Japanese missionary to "beat" poet, from "skinhead" Zen communalist and meditator to est seminarian, reflects the capacity of emergent spirituality, because it is emergent and its unities are largely invisible, to crop out in diverse ways. Swedenborgianism and Spiritualism expressed the excursus idea through the symbol of spirit worlds, and Theosophy in liminal pilgrimage. So did American Zen in pointing to what is inexpressible in wandering what is left of the North American wilderness, and in quiet sitting.

Epilogue

The Future of
Excursus Religion
in America

Changes in Critical Perspective

Books are still written which treat movements such as we have discussed as "cults of unreason" and as reactionary mysticisms which refuse to accept "science" and the new world it is creating. Certain of these books present useful empirical data, but the operative concepts of "reason" and "science" contained in them generally would have been simplistic in the heyday of logical positivism, and are vastly out of touch with the frontiers of philosophy of science, cosmology, physics, and psychological thought in the last quarter of the twentieth century. A classic Kuhnian paradigm shift is going on in these fields, basic to constructing the era's scientific master paradigms and world views. It is not so much a doctrinal battle as the simple replacement of one generation by another which does not think quite the same way: an older generation is still half in the world of Thomas Huxley, but a younger generation, more profoundly affected by the Einsteinian revolution in science on every level of attitude—including a new perception of the place of subjective consciousness in the cosmos wrought by its profound challenge to the "myth of the objective mind"—is sounding more like his contemporary Madame Blavatsky (at her best), or at least like Zen. (Outside of Jaina thought, I wonder if there is a better premodern anticipation of the philosophical dimensions of relativity theory than the essay on "Being-Time" by the thirteenth-century Japanese Zen master Dogen.) One should also mention a new openness by a new generation about parapsychological evidence regarding the nature of consciousness that approaches the same world, at least, as Swedenborgianism and Spiritualism.

Inevitably, this new mentality will lead to a more sympathetic understanding of the heritage of excursus religious movements and perhaps of the emergent tradition. It will not necessarily produce an adulation of them as having preternatural prescience (nor should it, for as does everything human they have their quotient of silliness), but perhaps it can be recognized that the sociological paradigms which lead people to perceive them only as "bizarre" and their members only as "cranks" are also capable of challenge and change. It can be perceived that these religions have not always been wrong or reactionary and that they have a place in the many-sided American spiritual symposium.

A perception of "non-normative" religions in America, even those imported (as it seems) from the East, as essentially American in America, and so to be understood (and criticized) in terms of the themes and sociology and styles of American religious life, involves another paradigm shift which is also under way. Zen, Swedenborgianism, Theosophy, or Vedanta, for example, are in American life far from what they are or were in Japan, eighteenth-century England, or nineteenth-century India. Too much knowledge of their distant origins, knowledge which may be greater than that of most twentieth-century American adherents themselves, can easily be a hindrance to comprehension of these adherents—who may use Eastern symbols, for reasons we have explored, but whose essential spiritual life is better approached through the American emergent and excursus heritage from Emerson, Thoreau, Whitman, the Shakers and Spiritualists, to the cults of the depression era, or to the "beatniks" and the "hippies."

Yet there are also books written which castigate American movements with Eastern links for failure to present the Eastern teaching in an "authentic" form and for adding to its classical texts "spurious" modern sources like the writings of Blavatsky. This sort of purist critique is, of course, legitimate within the context of commitment to the classic form of any tradition, but as applied to the phenomenology of religion it is unacceptable. Its ideal hardly fits the way religion really works, for religion is always in process, always undergoing modification through intercultural contact and trans-

plantation, and always producing new books which become normative and classical in time. Often, like the Mahayana sutras placed in
the mouth of the Buddha and the Tibetan *gter-ma* texts alleged to
have been penned by an ancient sage and hidden many centuries,
these classics are back-dated and ascribed to minds greater than
that of the one whose hands gave them to the world.

More important, as we have indicated, this attitude does little to
add to understanding of these movements in this country. If one is
going to talk about purity and authenticity of tradition (usually a
futile and dangerous project), one ought to talk about it in terms of
the American lineage in which a later phenomenon is placed. For
the "beat Zen" school, for example, the real ideal was clearly the
American ideal of Thoreau and Whitman, and of this Zen was
simply a new exotic symbol; it would make more sense (and be
more fair) to look at its values, life-style, and spirituality in that
light rather than to compare it with the Zen practiced long ago by
East Asian masters in a very different culture.

A contemporary genre of books exists whose chief purpose is to
indicate the alleged occult, theosophical, and oriental derivation of
the ideology of Nazism, and then to point with alarm to the
proliferation of those same teachings in America. It seems incum-
bent upon responsible writers of the history of such groups to point
out the logical and historical fallacies in this position, which, if
widely accepted, could have serious consequences for freedom of
religion.

First, it should be noted that, inasmuch as "the occult" only
joins Hegel, Wagner, Nietzsche, and the anti-Semitic strain in normative Christianity in receiving the blame for Hitlerism, one ought
finally to end up faulting not so much one small and easily identifiable culprit as a large part of the intellectual foundation of the
modern world.

Second, although the Theosophical doctrines of Madame Blavatsky and her followers are often cited in this connection, we should
note that whenever in modern history Theosophists have had a
discernible role and influence, as in the cultural renaissances and
independence movements of Ireland and India, it has been on the
side of freedom and democracy—and that leaders of the Theosophical Society, like many other occultists, disappeared into con-

centration camps in Germany as soon as the Nazis, their alleged disciples, came to power.

Third, let us reiterate that whatever meaning these ideologies may have in Asia or in Europe, in America they have appeared simply as revitalizations of a tradition going back as far as Transcendentalism, and usually aligned with the idealistic, even radical, wing of American democracy. To be sure, American occultism and non-normative religion can assume a rightist guise, and did to some extent in the 1930s. But this does not appear to be typical, or true to their historical roots. Despite superficial similarities, nothing is more different between Europe and America than the role of religion—both mainstream and non-normative—in the two societies. We must insist that American religious groups can only be judged in terms of American history, not in terms of any apparent European parallels, which inevitably will be misleading.

Time, as American culture matures and recognizes how unique it is (nowhere more so than in religion), will eventually provide its corrective on these points. Most American Eastern groups are now rapidly maturing—not in the direction of purism, but of indigenizing their own way; this is bound to happen more and more, even as it has with the Judaism and Christianity transplanted to these shores. The perception and appreciation of this process, and, thereby, the evaluation of excursus groups as integral parts of the American spiritual heritage, will be aided by the aforementioned changes in world-view paradigms. It will also be encouraged by the contemporary mood in religious studies, which by and large is far removed from the stereotyping and polemics of another day.

Changes in American Religion

One important reason for new attitudes in religious studies is new contours of American religion, and new perceptions by Americans of what their religion is. Most commentators in the late twentieth-century point to an increasing functional breakdown of what there was in America of the classic Troeltschean cleavage between church and sect, with an ever more radical exposure of more and more people to the extensive pluralism of American religion and a growing indifference to the large institutional structures of religion. In its place, one finds—in the flourishing of evangelicalism, pente-costalism, the "born again" experience, prayer groups, excursus religion, and para-religious self-realization activities like est—a movement toward subjectivity and small groups. This means, in our terms, that the structure of establishment religion, and the social identity that has gone with it, is crumbling. Indeed, the spiritual style and meaning that is associated with excursus religion is almost becoming normative, provided one includes its Judeo-Christian forms—a paradoxical situation whose ultimate cultural meaning is hard to assess. No model of a society whose religion is mainly subjective and small group (at best the local church or small intensive denomination), with no major religious institutions linked to the major institutions of government, business, and education, comes to mind which would be meaningfully com-parable to the United States.

That is certainly because this situation (which is not yet here, to be sure, but seems to be approaching), would be a product of modern social secularization, including those aspects of it which are genuinely unique to the contemporary era. Secularization unequiv-ocably does not mean decline in interest in religious issues or in desire for religious expression. That has obviously not been the upshot in the twentieth century. Rather, what it has meant is that religion has been increasingly divorced from the major structures of society—first (as early as the late Middle Ages) from economics, then from the state, then from education, and finally from religious institutions that parallel major structures of society in their organi-zation and symbolic social roles. That divorce liberates religion to exist principally, possibly even to prosper unprecedentedly, within subjectivity and in small groups.

American religion clearly is far better prepared to prosper in this situation, and to suffer fewer pains of transition to a new mode of life, than the religion of most societies. It has lived with secularism, in the sense suggested above, much longer than most other lands; and in its amazing pluralism, numerous religionists—not least those in our excursus religion—have experimented with and exper-ienced religion focused on private subjectivity and the small group rather than on the ecclesiastical institution. Indeed, we may expect to see our "non-normative" groups appear more and more normal, and even prestigious, at least from a sociological standpoint. It is hard to see how the new situation could bring them bane, and it could easily bring blessing.

But another way of looking at the picture (for there is little new under the sun in the history of religion) is that what is happening is simply a return to folk religion. It is a religion of Robert Redfield's "little tradition" of village and nonliterary folk transmission, excited as folk cultures are by the occasional thaumaturge or messiah, but without much vital interaction with the cultural "great tradition" of the society. Certainly there is much about American religion in the last quarter of the century which suggests this interpretation. It has no small vitality (folk religion, peasant culture religion, is often quite alive in terms of feeling and participation), but it has increasingly less real intellectual interaction with science, education, and the major institutions. As has been often remarked, there seem now to be no theological giants like Barth, Tillich, or the Niebuhrs capable of building bridges of serious dialogue between religion and culture. Instead, one senses that the issues being raised in the great tradition—the new cosmology, the medical revolution, present-day currents in literature and even social affairs —are very little engaged in by religion and vice versa. Religion, with the peasant's obstinate and almost deliberate naivete, is content to dwell with its own nonhistorical, and nonliterary—in the cultural sense—joys and apocalypses.

Probably that kind of religion is inevitable as a concomitant of the final divorce of religion from the major institutions, for folk or popular religion is that of a people largely separate from the major institutions of the society. As folk or popular religion usually does when first liberated from the grip of institutions, it will probably inflate and flourish to fill all the voids (as the evangelical tradition seems now to be doing), but that will still not commend it to the great tradition except for pro forma alliances.

But in the religious folk culture of a technological society, among the spiritual peasantry of a postindustrial nation, excursus religion could have a strange and important role. Every subjectivity, every small group, every charmed circle, needs the stimulus of something outside and different engaging it from time to time, lest it die of inertia. As American religion becomes more divorced from the great tradition, it receives less stimulus and engagement from that direction. Major intellectuals do not bother to address it, as Emerson and James once did, nor do they stir the ponds of its piety; neither is there any H. L. Mencken who troubles to bait it—though surely there are aspects of neo-evangelicalism worthy of his bite. But the two worlds, weary of each other and perhaps even of themselves as combatants, merely drift apart, until they become nearly invisible to each other.

Yet American religion is aware of the excursus, alternative tradition—it is something it can understand even in its present intellectual anemia as a competitor and challenger on its own turf. Through television and newspaper publicity, Spiritualism, Zen, other Eastern religions, and the like, are perceived as part of the religious scene—and perceived as rivals by those committed to the Judeo-Christian tradition. But in that very rivalry they can do what our highly nonmilitant secularism is far too bland to undertake— they can stimulate and challenge all American religion to think, to define its views of human nature, of the infinite and the spiritual path, in ways that take into account the experiences of others with other views and on other paths.

This they have done before, and can do again.

Notes

1   *Temple and Cave in America*

1.   Peter L. Berger, *The Sacred Canopy* (Garden City, N.Y.: Doubleday Anchor Books, 1969), p. 28.

2.   C. G. Jung, *Memories, Dreams, Reflections* (N.Y.: Pantheon Books, 1963), p. 39.

3.   J. Lofland and R. Stark, "Becoming a World-Saver: A Theory of Conversion to a Deviant Perspective," *American Sociological Review* 30 (1965): 862–74.

3.   J. Lofland and R. Stark, "Becoming a World-Saver: A Theory of Conversion to a Deviant Perspective," pp. 862–74. See also John Lofland, " 'Becoming a World-Saver' Revisited," *American Behavioral Scientist* 20, no. 6 (July-August 1977): 805–17; and James T. Richardson and Mary Stewart, "Conversion Process Models and the Jesus Movement," *American Behavioral Scientist* 20, no. 6 (July-August 1977): 819–38, especially p. 822, where the Lofland and Stark model is summarized.

4.   Robert Balch and David Taylor, "Seekers and Savers: The Role of the Cultic Milieu in Joining a UFO Cult," *American Behavioral Scientist* 20, no. 6 (July-August 1977): 839–60.

5.   Frederick R. Lynch, "Toward a Theory of Conversion and Commitment to the Occult," *American Behavioral Scientist* 20, no. 6 (July-August 1977): 887–908.

6.   Stephen C. Pepper, *World Hypotheses* (Berkeley and Los Angeles: University of California Press, 1942).

7.   For this discussion I am deeply indebted to a stimulating essay by Victor Turner, "Social Dramas and Ritual Metaphors," in *Dramas, Fields, and Metaphors* (Ithaca, N.Y.: Cornell University Press, 1974), pp. 23–59.

8.   Paul Radin, *Primitive Man as Philosopher* (New York: Dover Publications, 1957).

9.   Turner, *Dramas, Fields, and Metaphors*, pp. 24–25. Robert A.

Nisbet, *Social Change and History: Aspects of the Western Theory of Development* (London: Oxford University Press, 1969), pp. 3-4.

10.   J. Milton Yinger, *Religion, Society, and the Individual* (New York: Macmillan, 1957), pp. 142-55.

11.   Geoffrey K. Nelson, *Spiritualism and Society* (New York: Schocken Books, 1969), p. 220. In a more recent book, *The Scientific Study of Religion* (New York: Macmillan, 1970), pp. 279-80, J. Milton Yinger discusses and generally accepts Nelson's contention that some cults can be long-lasting and the sources of new religions.

12.   James T. Richardson, ''An Oppositional and General Conceptualization of Cult.'' Unpublished paper read at the annual meeting of the Association for the Sociology of Religion (New York, 1976), p. 7.

13.   Roy Wallis, ''Ideology, Authority and the Development of Cultic Movements,'' *Social Research* 41, no. 2 (Summer 1974): 299-327.

2   *Excursus Religion*

1.   Cited and translated in W. R. Irwin, ''There and Back Again: The Romances of Williams, Lewis, and Tolkien,'' *Sewanee Review* 64, no. 4 (Oct.-Dec. 1961): 566.

2.   Irwin, ''There and Back Again,'' p. 567.

3.   Mary Douglas, *Natural Symbols* (New York: Vintage Books, 1973).

4.   Sheldon R. Isenberg and Dennis E. Owen, ''Bodies, Natural and Contrived: The Work of Mary Douglas,'' *Religious Studies Review* 3, no. 1 (January 1977): 7-8. The following table is reprinted by permission of the authors.

5.   Isenberg and Owen, ''Bodies, Natural and Contrived,'' p. 14.

6.   Victor W. Turner, *The Ritual Process* (Chicago: Aldine, 1969).

7.   Frederick J. Streng, *Understanding Religious Man* (Belmont, Calif.: Dickenson, 1969), pp. 4-5.

8.   Douglas, *Natural Symbols*, p. 190.

9.   Isenberg and Owen, ''Bodies, Natural and Contrived,'' p. 14.

10.   Joachim Wach, *Sociology of Religion* (Chicago: University of Chicago Press, 1944), pp. 17-34.

11.   Erving Goffman, *Asylums: Essays on the Social Situation of Mental Patients and Other Inmates* (Garden City, N.Y.: Doubleday Anchor Books, 1961).

12.   Troeltsch, *Social Teachings of the Christian Church*, 2:734. See also William R. Garrett, ''Maligned Mysticism: The Maledicted Career of Troeltsch's Third Type,'' *Sociological Analysis* 36, no. 3 (1975): 205-27. Garrett argues cogently that Troeltsch's mysticism type—shifted by Max Weber into a coordinate on the asceticism-mysticism axis *within* church and sect—deserves instead to be looked at anew as a third religious *type* and as such to be factored into the sociology of religion afresh.

13.   Robert S. Ellwood, Jr., "Notes on a Neo-Pagan Religious Group in America," *History of Religions* 11, no. 1 (August 1971): 125-39; and Robert S. Ellwood, Jr., *Religious and Spritual Groups in Modern America* (Englewood Cliffs, N.J.: Prentice-Hall, 1973), pp. 194-200.

14.   Peter L. Berger and Thomas Luckmann, *The Social Construction of Reality* (Garden City, N.Y.: Doubleday Anchor Books, 1967).

3   Inner Worlds   The Psychology of Excursus Religion

1.   Godfré Ray King [Guy Ballard], *Unveiled Mysteries* (Chicago: Saint Germain Press, 1939), p. 2.

2.   Paul Twitchell, *The Tiger's Fang* (New York: Lancer Books, 1969), p. 13.

3.   Carl G. Jung, *Flying Saucers: A Modern Myth of Things Seen in the Sky* (New York: Signet Books, 1969), pp. 119-26.

4.   Orfeo M. Angelucci, *The Secret of the Saucers* (Amherst, Wisc.: Amherst Press, 1955), pp. 1-5.

5.   Alfred Schutz, *Collected Papers*, vol. 1, edited and with an introduction by Maurice Natanson (The Hague: Martinus Nijhoff, 1973), pp. 207-59. See also William James, *The Principles of Psychology*, vol. 2, chap. 21 (New York: H. Holt and Co., 1890).

6.   Ralph W. Hood, Jr., "Eliciting Mystical States of Consciousness with Semistructured Nature Experiences," *Journal for the Scientific Study of Religion* 16, no. 2 (1977): 199-263.

7.   See in particular R. D. Laing, *The Politics of Experience* (New York: Ballantine Books, 1967).

8.   R. D. Laing, "Metanoia: Some Experiences at Kingsley Hall, London," in Hendrick M. Ruitenbeek, ed., *Going Crazy: The Radical Therapy of R. D. Laing and Others* (New York: Bantam Books, 1972), pp. 16-19. See also an essay by the woman who regressed herself in the same books: Mary Barnes, "Flection-Reflection," pp. 103-18.

9.   Laing, *The Politics of Experience*, p. 157.

10.   Robert S. Ellwood, Jr., *Religious and Spritual Groups in Modern America* (Englewood Cliffs, N.J.: Prentice-Hall, 1973), pp. 49-52, passim.

11.   Vsevolod Gergyeevich Solovyoff, *A Modern Priestess of Isis*, translated by Walter Leaf (London: Longmans, Green, 1895; reprint ed. New York: Arno Press, 1976), pp. 176-81.

12.   Heinrich Zimmer, *Myths and Symbols in Indian Art and Civilization* (New York: Bollengen Foundation, 1946), p. 179, note. I am indebted for this quote and for the basic insight here discussed regarding the trickster and the counter-spirituality personality to a letter by Melanie Bandy in *The American Theosophist* 65, no. 11 (November 1977): 315.

13.   Ernest G. Schachtel, "On Memory and Childhood Amnesia," in his *Metamorphosis: On the Development of Affect, Perception, Attention, and Memory* (New York: Basic Books, 1959), pp. 279-322. See especially pp. 298-301.

14.   Kenneth Grant, *The Magical Revival* (New York: Samuel Weiser, 1973), p. 3.

4   *Shakers and Spiritualists*

1.   From Eirik's Saga, in Magnus Magnusson and Hermann Palsson, *The Vinland Sagas* (New York: New York University Press, 1966), pp. 81-84.

2.   Magnusson and Palsson, *The Vinland Sagas*, pp. 64-67, 71.

3.   I. M. Lewis, *Ecstatic Religion* (Harmondsworth, England: Penguin Books, 1971), p. 31.

4.   Lines found in her sketch-book, undated. Cited in Mary K. Neff, comp., *Personal Memoirs of H. P. Blavatsky* (Wheaton, Ill.: Theosophical Publishing House, 1937), p. 37.

5.   Carl Carmer, *Listen for a Lonesome Drum* (New York: William Sloane Associates, 1936), pp. 203-14.

6.   *Testimonies of the Life, Character, Revelations and Doctrines of Mother Ann Lee* (Albany: Weed Parsons, 1888. Reprint ed., New York: AMS Press, 1975), p. 5.

7.   *Testimonies of the Life . . . of Mother Ann Lee*, in Marguerite Fellows Melcher, *The Shaker Adventure* (Princeton: Princeton University Press, 1941), passim.

8.   Cited in Frederick William Evans, *Autobiography of a Shaker* (New York: American News Company, 1888; reprint ed. New York: AMS Press, 1973), pp. 268-69.

9.   Hester M. Poole, "Shakers and Shakerism," in Evans, *Autobiography of a Shaker*, p. 268.

10.   J. M. Peebles, "Cycles," in Evans, *Autobiography of a Shaker*, p. 115.

11.   Melcher, *The Shaker Adventure*, p. 185.

12.   Melcher, *The Shaker Adventure*, p. 217. See also Edward Deming Andrews and Faith Andrews, *Fruits of the Shaker Tree of Life* (Stockbridge, Mass.: The Berkshire Traveller Press, 1975), especially pp. 220-21.

13.   Evans, *Autobiography of a Shaker*, p. 43.

14.   Evans, *Autobiography of a Shaker*, pp. 18-20.

15.   Carl Carmer, *Listen for a Lonesome Drum*, pp. 145-46. Whitney R. Cross, *The Burned Over District: The Social and Intellectual History of Enthusiastic Religion in Western New York* (New York: Harper and Row), 1965.

16.   George Trobridge, *Swedenborg: Life and Teaching* (New York: Swedenborg Foundation, 1935), p. 118.

17.   "Emanuel Swedenborg," translated by Richard Howard and César Rennert. Excerpted from the book *Jorge Luis Borges: Selected Poems 1923–1967,* edited by Norman Thomas di Giovanni. English translation copyright © 1968, 1970, 1971, 1972 by Emece Editores, S. A., and Norman Thomas di Giovanni. Reprinted by permission of Delacorte Press/Seymour Lawrence and Penguin Books, Ltd.

18.   See Robert Price, *Johnny Appleseed: Man and Myth.* (Gloucester, Mass.: Peter Smith, 1967).

19.   An accessible work on Mesmer, with good bibliography, is Vincent Buranelli, *The Wizard from Vienna* (New York: Coward, McCann and Geoghegan, 1975). On Mesmerism in America as it led up to Spiritualism see Slater Brown, *The Heyday of Spiritualism* (New York: Hawthorn Books, 1970).

20.   Catherine L. Albanese, *Corresponding Motion: Transcendental Religion and the New America.* Philadelphia: Temple University Press, 1977.

21.   The primary source is Andrew Jackson Davis, *The Magic Staff: An Autobiography* (New York: J. S. Brown and Co., 1857). See also Brown, *The Heyday of Spiritualism,* chap. 7.

22.   A fascinating though non-critical biography is Jean Burton, *Heyday of a Wizard* (New York: A. A. Knopf, 1944).

23.   Brown, *The Heyday of Spiritualism,* chap. 12.

24.   Whitney Cross, *The Burned Over District,* p. 348. One feels that the meteoric rise and fall of Spiritualism as a major cultural phenomenon in the 1850s, together with its ongoing influence through subdued but continuing institutions and in the lives of people who had seen their "literal-mindedness and orthodoxy" obliterated in its embrace, strikingly parallels the course and probable destiny of the "counterculture" religion of the 1960s. Both were linked with social radicalism, Amerindian lore, and wild eschatological visions; both seemed to vanish as sensational news only a few years after they had come, and were dampened by more sober forms of liberal and evangelical religion and a more pragmatic vision of society, which appeared in the seventies of both centuries. Yet over twelve decades later one can trace directly back to the first Spiritualist outburst a variety of lively activities from Theosophy to serious psychical research, and perceive an indirect influence on the rise of modern psychology and liberalism of several sorts. One should not foreclose the possibility of an equally subtle but far-reaching influence of Haight-Ashbury, for all its apparent ephemerality, on the twenty-first century.

On the relation of Spiritualism to rationalistic modernism, so evident in the thought of Frederick Evans the Shaker and many others, one may reflect on these words of Mircea Eliade:

I noticed long ago that spiritualism is the "spiritual" compensation that positivism allows itself. When one can no longer *believe* (in the Judeo-Christian sense of the term), one needs *concrete proofs* of the survival of the soul; it is on the basis of these "experimental" proofs that an after life is constructed—with its structures and its hierarchies—just as theologies are constructed (in a monotheistic climate) on the basis of a few prophetic revelations and mystical experiences.

Mircea Eliade, *No Souvenirs: Journal 1957-1969*. Translated from the French by Fred H. Johnson, Jr. (New York: Harper and Row, 1977), p. 145.

25.   See Herbert W. Schneider and George Lawton, *A Pilgrim and a Prophet: Being the Incredible History of Thomas Lake Harris and Laurence Oliphant* (New York: Columbia University Press, 1942).

26.   Howard Kerr, *Mediums, and Spirit-Rappers, and Roaring Radicals: Spiritualism in American Literature 1850-1900* (Urbana: University of Illinois Press, 1972).

27.   Henry S. Olcott, *People from the Other World* (Hartford: American Publishing Co., 1875; reprint ed. Rutland, Vt.: Charles E. Tuttle Company, 1972), p. 481.

5   *Olcott and Blavatsky*
                                                Journey to the East

1.   Letter by Madame Blavatsky in the *Spiritual Scientist* (Boston), vol. 1, December 3, 1874, pp. 148-49. Excerpted in *H. P. Blavatsky: Collected Writings, 1874-78*, vol. 1 (Adyar, Madras, India: Theosophical Publishing House, 1966), p. 47.

2.   The principal source for the plagiarism charge is the time-consuming work which William Emmett Coleman did around the turn of the century to substantiate some 2000 plagiarisms in *Isis Unveiled*. His findings were published with full references in a series of magazine articles, and summarized in "The Sources of Madame Blavatsky's Writings" (appendix C to V. S. Solovyoff, *A Modern Priestess of Isis,* previously cited). Bruce Campbell, of the Institute of Religious Studies, University of California, Santa Barbara, has recently checked a substantial sample of these alleged borrowings. He concluded that the 2000 plagiarisms do exist, but are nearly all on the level of sentences and phrases in the midst of unplagiarized discourse, and so in a work of some 1400 pages probably do not represent more than five percent or so of the total. He did not find even this much plagiarism in *The Secret Doctrine*.

A curious light is shed on the whole business by the fact that the British Museum catalog lists an 1881 publication by William Henry Burr, a religious controversalist, devoted to accusing W. E. Coleman himself of plagiarism from his "Sunday Not the Sabbath."

3.   Given in Mary K. Neff, comp., *Personal Memoirs of H. P. Blavat-sky* (Wheaton, Ill.: Theosophical Publishing House, 1937), pp. 341–42. Originally from Mrs. E. Johnson, "Letters of H. P. Blavatsky," *The Path*, December, 1894.

4.   Neff, *Personal Memoirs*, pp. 236–40.

5.   Gertrude M. Williams, *Priestess of the Occult* (New York: Alfred A. Knopf, 1946), passim.

6.   Henry Steel Olcott, *Old Diary Leaves: America 1874–1878, first series* (Adyar, Madras, India: Theosophical Publishing House, 1895) pp. 331–32. This volume henceforth cited as *ODL 1*.

7.   From the same letter cited in note 1, above.

8.   *ODL 1*, pp. 211–12.

9.   *ODL 1*, pp. 208–9.

10.   H. P. Blavatsky, *Isis Unveiled* (Wheaton, Ill.: Theosophical Publishing House, 1972 edition), 1:xi.

11.   It would be amiss not to mention here Helena Blavatsky's major work, *The Secret Doctrine* (1888), even though its composition comes after the period we are examining. The writing of this book seems to have been, as in the case of *Isis Unveiled*, a combination of psychic revelation and collective editorial effort by a circle of associates of the authoress to arrange her material. But *The Secret Doctrine* is much superior in sophistication and systematization; this is due partly to the high caliber of the later assistants, and partly, of course, to HPB's own maturation over the inter-vening decade. For fascinating firsthand accounts of the writing of *The Secret Doctrine*, see Countess Constance Wachtmeister et al., *Remi-niscences of H. P. Blavatsky and The Secret Doctrine* (Wheaton, Ill.: Theosophical Publishing House, 1976). A standard edition of the work, an-notated, indexed, and containing the posthumous third volume on sym-bolism, whose authorship by HPB is disputed, is H. P. Blavatsky, *The Secret Doctrine*, 6 vols. (Adyar, Madras, India: Theosophical Publishing House; sixth Adyar edition, 1971).

12.   See Neff, *Personal Memoirs*, pp. 282, 289. In connection with HPB's relation to Russian Orthodoxy, it has sometimes been suggested there was something very Russian about her "mysticism," that she was more of an occultist *startsi* than anything else. While her psychic and mystic performances may have owed much to the *startsi* and other Eastern spiritual traditions, this does not seem to me to be the case in regard to the intellectual expression of her mysticism. Her maiden name was de Hahn, and on her father's side she was descended from German immigrants to Russia, though her mother, a gifted novelist, was of the old princely Dolgouroky house. However, HPB's world was that of those nineteenth-century Russian aristocrats more German in race and French in culture than Russian; despite her Russophile side, this is what comes through in her doctrine. In *Isis, The Secret Doctrine,* and her other writings, there is very little of the sensuous Slavic mysticism of guilt and joy, of love of the divine

in the humble, the suffering, and the soil, which lends passion to almost every page of Dostoevsky, Solovyov, and Blok, and gives spiritual character even to a figure like Rasputin, despite the fact she shared many of these passions in her own tempestuous life. Rather, hers seems doctrinally a much more Germanic style of mysticism. It has clearer affinities to the more intellectual, system-building occultism of the German Renaissance, to Paracelsus, Rosicrucianism, and Boehme, than to Russia. Despite its parallelism to the Platonic theology of the Eastern Church, her Platonism seems to be more that of the kabbala and the Rhineland than of Byzantium. On top of this, there is something of the flavor of the more recent French Spiritualism of Saint-Martin and Kardec.

13.   John Symonds, *Madame Blavatsky, Medium and Magician* (London: Odhams Press, 1959), p. 103. Gertrude Williams (*Priestess of the Occult*, p. 130) believed that, together with her congenital wanderlust, the humiliation of Home's book was the strongest reason for HPB's decision to go to India.

14.   Neff, *Personal Memoirs*, p. 55.

15.   Williams, *Priestess of the Occult*, pp. 89–90.

16.   "The Diaries of H. P. Blavatsky," 1878, in H. P. Blavatsky, *Collected Writings*, 1:414–15.

17.   Ibid., p. 420.

18.   *ODL 1*, pp. 17–18.

19.   *ODL 1*, pp. 376–77, 379.

20.   Henry Steel Olcott, *Old Diary Leaves, 1878–83, second series* (Adyar, Madras, India: Theosophical Publishing House, 1900), pp. 13–14. This volume henceforth cited as *ODL 2*.

21.   Victor Turner, "The Center Out There: Pilgrim's Goal," *History of Religions* 12, no. 3 (February 1973): 191–230.

22.   Henry David Thoreau, *Journal* (New York: Dover Publications, 1962), 8:134.

23.   Henry David Thoreau, *Walden* (New York: New American Library, 1942), pp. 198–99.

24.   *ODL 2:* 21, 24–25.

25.   See the excellent biography, Mary Lutyens, *Krishnamurti: The Years of Awakening* (New York: Farrar, Straus, and Giroux, 1975).

6   *Zen Journeys to the West*

1.   *The International Theosophical Yearbook 1937* (Adyar, Madras, India: Theosophical Publishing House), p. 151, tells of Mrs. Suzuki's establishing the Mahayana Lodge of Theosophists in Kyoto in 1924, and of her "enthusiastic work" in spreading Theosophy in Japan. Both Suzukis greeted Theosophical visitors to the island empire, including the international president, C. Jinarajadasa, in 1937.

2.   Mircea Eliade, *No Souvenirs* (New York: Harper and Row, 1977), p. 208. For an interesting assessment by Conze of D. T. Suzuki and Western Zen see Edward Conze, *Thirty Years of Buddhist Studies* (Columbia, S.C.: University of South Carolina Press, 1968), pp. 27-32.

3.   Alan W. Watts, *Beat Zen, Square Zen, and Zen* (San Francisco: City Lights Books, 1959). This essay contains an interesting critique of Jack Kerouac's *The Dharma Bums*.

4.   Heinrich Dumoulin, S. J., *A History of Zen Buddhism* (Boston: Beacon Press, 1969), pp. 184-86.

5.   Jack Kerouac, *The Dharma Bums* (New York: Viking Press, 1958), pp. 72-77.

6.   Kerouac, *The Dharma Bums*, p. 84.

7.   Kerouac, *The Dharma Bums*, p. 243.

8.   Ann Charters, *Kerouac* (New York: Warner Paperback Library Edition, 1974), pp. 217-31. This book is the standard biography of Jack Kerouac.

9.   David Kherdian, *A Biographical Sketch and Descriptive Checklist of Gary Snyder* (Berkeley: Oyez Press, 1965).

10.   Gary Snyder, *Riprap and Cold Mountain Poems* (San Francisco: City Lights Books, 1958), pp. 39-40.

11.   Quoted in David Kherdian, *Six Poets of the San Francisco Renaissance* (Fresno, Calif.: The Gilgia Press, 1965), p. 52.

12.   Gary Snyder, *Earth House Hold* (New York: New Directions, 1969), p. 132.

13.   Personal Communication, May 23, 1977.

14.   Alan Watts, *In My Own Way: An Autobiography, 1915-65* (New York: Vintage Books, 1973), p. 309.

15.   Alan W. Watts, *The Way of Zen* (New York: Pantheon Books, 1957), p. 3.

16.   Gary Snyder, interview statement in *Wind Bell,* publication of the San Francisco Zen Center, 8 nos. 1-2 (Fall 1969): 29. Reprinted by permission.

17.   Reprinted by permission from *Wind Bell,* 8 nos. 1-2 (Fall 1969): 1.

18.   Undated manuscript cited in Louis Nordstrom, ed., *Namu Dai Bosa: A Transmission of Zen Buddhism to America.* (New York: Theatre Arts Books, 1976), pp. 58-59.

19.   *Wind Bell* 8, nos. 1-2 (Fall 1969): 2-3. I am deeply indebted to this invaluable issue of the publication of the San Francisco Zen Center for much of the material on the history of formal Zen in America presented in this chapter.

20.   Biography based on *Wind Bell* 11 (1972): 7-10.

21.   *Wind Bell* 9, nos. 3-4 (Fall-Winder 1970-71): 39-40.

22.   Wilfred Cantwell Smith, *Religious Diversity,* ed. Willard G. Oxtoby (New York: Harper and Row, 1976). See especially the essay,

"Religiously Divided History Approaches Self-Consciousness," pp. 96–116.
23.   Adelaide Bry, *Est: 60 Hours that Transform your Life* (New York: Harper and Row, 1976), p. 115.

Index